POPULATIONS IN DANGER 1995

BOOKS BY MÉDECINS SANS FRONTIÈRES

Populations in Danger 1995, A Médecins Sans Frontières Report:
edited by François Jean, Médecins Sans Frontières, 1995.
Life, Death and Aid, The Médecins Sans Frontières Report on
World Crisis Intervention: edited by François Jean, Routledge,
1993.
Populations in Danger: edited by François Jean, John Libbey, 1992.

English language edition first published 1995
by Médecins Sans Frontières (UK)
124-132 Clerkenwell Rd.
London EC1R 5DL
copyright La Découverte 1995
Printed and bound in France by La Découverte
British Library Cataloguing in Publication Data
A catalogue record for this book is available from the British Library
Library of Congress Cataloging in Publication Data
Has been applied for
ISBN 0-9525057-0-3

Populations in danger 1995

A *Médecins Sans Frontières* Report

Edited by François Jean

AUTHORS

Five crises

ean-Pierre CHRÉTIEN, François JEAN, Béatrice POULIGNY, Marc
ΛO, Jean-Claude WILLAME.

Opinion

Rony BRAUMAN, Philippe CHABASSE, Guy HERMET, Erwann
QUEINNEC, Alain MOREN, Jean RIGAL, Françoise BOUCHET-
SAULNIER.
All of the above are members of Médecins Sans Frontières.
Philippe Chabasse is also co-director of Handicap International.

The humanitarian atlas

Virginie RAISSON, with the contribution of Laurence CAPITAINE,
Mathilde CORONAT, Frank TETART, Sonia RAISSON and
Jean-Christophe VICTOR.
Maps produced by the Paris-based Laboratoire d'études
politiques et d'analyses cartographiques (LEPAC).

Inserts: Hervé DEGUINE, Abdel Rahman GHANDOUR, Patrick
GUIBERT, François JEAN, Michel KASSA, Pierre SALIGNON and
Patrick VIAL.

English edition : Iseult O'BRIEN

CONTENTS

FOREWORD

Alain Destexhe,
Secretary General of the international office
of Médecins Sans Frontières

The construction of a new world order and the development of the United Nations (UN) organization since the Second World War have been guided by the principle: Never Again. The Nazis' unprecedented crime against the Jews became a benchmark for an international community founded on certain basic values: opposition to genocide, the search for world peace and respect for human rights. In 1948, the UN General Assembly adopted a convention committing member countries to punish and prevent genocide. Now, only fifty years later, the world has failed to react to the first indisputable genocide since that perpetrated against the Jews. It has stood back and allowed between half a million and a million people to be massacred with impunity simply because they were born Tutsis.

Genocide and humanitarian aid

The victims of the massacres that began on 6 April, immediately after the death of the Rwandese president, Juvénal Habyarimana, initially included both Hutus and Tutsis. There was, however, one fundamental difference; whereas Hutus belonging to the democratic opposition or human rights organisations were murdered for their political convictions, Tutsis were slaughtered simply for being Tutsis.
A genocide is an exceptional event in 20th-century history. The term was first used in 1944 to qualify the massive crimes against humanity committed by the Nazis in Occupied Europe. Since then the word genocide has so often been misused in attempts to grab attention by drawing parallels with the crime of the century that it has become synonymous with any act of mass murder.
And yet, genocide is defined not by the number of victims or the cruelty of the act, but solely by the deliberate intention to exterminate a national, ethnic, racial or religious group. The crime

is characterised by the targeting of a specific group for no other reason than its very existence. As the etymology suggests, the term does not apply to politically-defined groups, but exclusively to those constituted by race, ethnicity, nationality or religion. The term can therefore be applied to few situations this century, and certainly not to all those that it has been used to describe, among them the Vietnam War, Biafra, Cambodia and Somalia.

The punishment and prevention of genocide were among the new foundations underpinning the post-war international community. By attempting to wipe entire groups off the face of the earth — denying entire peoples the right to live alongside other people — genocide was by definition a universal issue. Analysing the Eichmann Trial in Jerusalem, Hannah Arendt summed it up as follows: "Extermination of whole ethnic groups — the Jews, or the Poles, or the Gipsies — was more than a crime against the Jewish or the Polish or the Gipsy people, ... the international order, and mankind in its entirety, had been grievously hurt and endangered." She felt that "if genocide is an actual possibility in the future, then no people on earth ... can feel reasonably sure of its continued existence without the help and protection of international law". The 1948 Convention on genocide is considered part of international customary law, i.e. binding on all states, be they signatories or not.

In spite of this the world did absolutely nothing to forestall the eradication of the Tutsis in Rwanda. Indeed it was a long time before it would even classify what was happening as genocide. The initial reaction was to give up and pull out, with compassion and humanitarian aid following somewhat belatedly. In a world sometimes described as a "global village" with instantaneous communications, it is still possible to kill between half a million and a million people without any international reaction. At best, the international community failed to understand that this was no ordinary crisis but an absolutely exceptional occurrence; at worst, obsessed by its setback in Somalia, it did not want to take even the slightest of risks.

Widespread indifference

The simple fact that it was possible, in 1994, to commit genocide amid widespread indifference raises grave questions about the constraints placed by the world on the instigators and perpetrators of mass murder.

First, what does "international community" mean? This vague notion of belonging to a community of nations, entailing rights, responsibilities and rules of conduct, has been evolving since the 16th century. It began to pick up speed with the setting up of the League of Nations, acquiring still greater momentum after 1945 through the UN. As the end of the century nears, this community might reasonably be expected to at least protect its members when they find themselves the target of radical extermination attempts. This did not happen in Rwanda. France's belated intervention showed that the Tutsis could have been saved. Had such an operation been conducted earlier and across a larger area, the lives of tens of thousands of people seeking refuge in churches, stadiums and schools would have been spared.

Second, the UN, and above all the major powers involved, placed the instigators of the genocide and the Rwandese Patriotic Front (RPF) on the same footing; once again they delayed before taking sides, and once again their intervention — after between half a million and a million people had died — came in the form of humanitarian aid for the Hutu refugees, the Tutsis inside Rwanda having been almost entirely wiped out. Humanitarian action is playing an increasingly ambiguous role in international crises. While one can only rejoice at the massive sympathy inspired throughout the world by the human catastrophe of the Hutu exodus, itself organized by the genocide's perpetrators, this wave of human feeling came when the genocide had been accomplished. This praiseworthy mobilization was not, however, without side-effects. It pushed the genocide into the background, wiping away the shame of the initial failure to act and giving the world something to feel good about. It is increasingly becoming a feature of modern society that anything goes as long as a few firemen are allowed to fling the occasional bucket of relief at the political house fire.

Finally, justice may well become a political imperative. It is necessary not only for the victims, but also for international order. Not to judge the perpetrators and instigators of the genocide would not only be a terrible injustice, but a grave political error. There is enormous potential in the world today for crises with an ethnic dimension to take place. The greatest threat to society internationally is the rebirth of racist ideologies, with their racial hierarchies that reject and exclude all others. From Burma to Sudan, the Caucasus to the former Yugoslavia, Bosnia and Zaire, such racism is flourishing. If the international community allows these ideologies to provoke genocide, relief organisations will be left helpless. Only political action and the punishment of mass murderers will offer any hope of making leaders think twice before playing the ethnic card to tighten their slackening grip on power. The special tribunal for former Yugoslavia will be the first test of international determination; the second will be the fate of the small clique close to President Habyarimana, who planned and organized the extermination of the Tutsis.

Confronting crises

Hot on the heels of Bosnia and Somalia, the Rwandese crisis bears out the major trend discernible in the management of international crises. The honeymoon period, that began with the end of the Cold War and the dreams of a "New World Order", seems to be over. The major powers have made it clear that the UN is not going to be the world's policeman, and that none of them, the United States included, is able or willing to take on the job. After a period of rapid expansion, peacekeeping operations have come to a halt. Rwanda was the first time that the international organization responded to a crisis not by stepping up its involvement but by a brutal disengagement, cutting the UN Assistance Mission to Rwanda (UNAMIR) forces from 2, 500 to 270. The US has, moreover, learned from its failure in Somalia: the Clinton administration's recent directive on peacekeeping operations limits the scope for intervention. The new policy is aimed at avoiding US involvement in regions where it has no strategic interests and reducing the US share in financing the UN. These new guidelines, which hamstring the UN, can be summarized as follows: the US will veto any further deployment of peacekeeping forces unless certain conditions (logistical, financial and the like) are satisfied; in practice, these conditions cannot be satisfied without the backing of the US. The Tutsis were the first to suffer the consequences of this new policy. Yet every situation is different. Rwanda is not Somalia, and the concept of intervention should not be abandoned forever just because the US lost 30 professional soldiers on the shores of the Indian Ocean.

Brought about by the relative retreat of the UN, there is a now discernible trend towards the regionalization of peace-keeping. Thus, Russia has been given the go-ahead by the UN to intervene on its behalf in what it terms the near abroad, in particular Georgia, while France went it alone in Rwanda. The US, for its part, was given permission to land in Haiti. In Liberia, the regional intervention forces are heavily dominated by heavyweight Nigeria, and in Bosnia the UN is politically far behind the "contact group" of mediators, the US, Russia, Britain, France and Germany. This was recognized by Mr. Boutros-Ghali when he proposed in a letter to the Security

Council, that UN forces be withdrawn regardless of whether the warring parties accepted the proposals of the "contact group", and asked the group to assume responsibility for both the political management of the crisis and peacekeeping.

This trend in the international response to crises is a throwback to the 19th-century diplomatic set up, with its spheres of influence, "legitimate interests" and gunboat diplomacy. There is, however, one crucial difference: those intervening first ask for the UN's approval, which not only confers much greater legitimacy on their actions, but also gives the impression that they are subcontractors working for the UN. This trend may seem realistic, given the refusal of the major powers to set up a UN standing army, but it is worrying nonetheless. First, it raises even more bluntly the question of just how impartial such intervention is. Second, it harks back to a sometimes inglorious past (France in Rwanda, the US in Haiti and Russia in the Commonwealth of Independent States [CIS]). Last, but far from least, it may mean abandoning people in whom no major power has even a selfish interest.

Migration plays a part

This trend also shows the importance of patterns of migration in the determination of international policy. If the US or UN is intervening in Haiti, it is not due to the country's internal problems or the lack of democracy, but because of migration from the island. Cuba presents similar problems, and such considerations are not irrelevant to the formulation of Russian policy towards CIS countries with sizeable Russian minorities, where any explosions of violence could result in considerable population movements. Even in the case of tiny Rwanda, a massive exodus risks destabilizing the frail Zairian giant, something that the Western powers would not be indifferent to. The desire to keep refugees within the frontiers of the former Yugoslavia accounts to a large extent for European policy on this crisis.

In the former Yugoslavia, Médecins Sans Frontières has repeatedly attacked the strictly humanitarian approach prevalent since the conflict started. Coming after Srebrenica and Gorazde, the siege of Bihac is just a further illustration of the powerlessness of the UN — and now of NATO. There is a repeated talk of withdrawing the peacekeeping forces. Yet aid to the victims is not negotiable, it is a moral obligation quite independent of the success of any political settlement. The subsequent failure of any such settlement would not be a valid excuse for the UN and the European Union to abandon or reduce their relief efforts, which must continue regardless of the political situation, as long as people are suffering. The European Union has for a long time limited its involvement to relief work. Were it to stop or reduce its aid on the pretext that the parties had failed to reach agreement, it would only underline the hypocrisy and cynicism of its earlier policy.

With Médecins Sans Frontières' third publication for the International Day for Populations in Danger, the organization is continuing its efforts to draw attention to people in hardship and consider humanitarian work in its wider context. Considerable space is given to the question of genocide. At the risk of neglecting other major tragedies, especially those receiving little or no media coverage, we nonetheless consider it essential to stress the singular nature of genocide and the questions such a crime raises for the international community.

Despite the conscious decision this year to focus on crises that have already made some impact on public opinion, Médecins Sans Frontières continues to carry out most of its work in forgotten conflicts. Despite the rather distorted impression conveyed by media coverage of humanitarian dramas, some successes are worth emphasising. Tensions have been reduced in several regions of the world, even if many problems remain unresolved. Several years ago Central America, South Africa, Mozambique and South-East Asia had the dubious honour of figuring highly on any shortlist of political crises or human dramas. Of course these countries still have serious problems, but the level of violence is not what it was. In Mozambique the peace process is running behind schedule and remains fragile, but it is continuing. In Cambodia, the Khmers Rouges have stepped up operations, but are not perceived as a political or military alternative to the present government. In El Salvador, the death squads have resumed work, but vital progress has been made towards national reconciliation in a country ravaged by fourteen years of civil war. It would be wrong to give way to an artificial pessimism induced by a succession of tragedies publicized by the media. And the common assertion that there are more wars or disasters than twenty years ago should at least be seriously examined.

However distressed we may be by tragedies such as Yugoslavia or Rwanda, we should remember that there have been crises on a similar scale in the past. The war that followed the Soviet invasion of Afghanistan displaced more than five million people, while Bangladesh's declaration of independence in 1971 and the ensuing repression caused nearly ten million people to flee to neighbouring

India within weeks. The Rwandese exodus may be the fastest ever, but it is certainly not the largest. The last twenty years have seen considerable improvement in the speed and efficiency of the humanitarian response to such crises, showing just how much progress has been made on the technical side. However, the serious political consequences of these crises were not tackled from a purely humanitarian standpoint, as is the case today.

If certain regions of the world are today at peace, many countries are still in the throes of war. Although several rural areas are enjoying relative stability, the Afghan conflict which long symbolized the Cold War drags on, indeed it is hotting up, particularly around the capital. In Sri Lanka, the war is now in its thirteenth year, and while there is a military stand-off of sorts, the number of civilian victims remains high. In Angola, whenever there is a let-up in international pressure, the warring parties multiply the obstacles in the way of humanitarian work, with many besieged cities regularly cut off from all aid for months. The war in Angola is a classic example of how media coverage can influence the behaviour of the warring parties and can affect access to the victims. In Sudan, the situation remains very serious and the obstacles to humanitarian aid continue to multiply. The Khartum government is pressing on with its policy of forced Islamization of all areas of society, while conducting a diplomatic charm offensive in the West, that regrettably seems to be bearing fruit. In the Caucasus, Zaire and Burma, a policy of "ethnic cleansing" is pursued, to general indifference. In Liberia, there is still no sign of a political solution and, what is worse, nobody seems to be looking for one. In these conflicts, and many others besides, Médecins Sans Frontières' teams are working to bring a little humanity to civilian victims of war or mischance.

The emergency ethic

All over the world, there is unprecedented enthusiasm for humanitarian work. It is far from certain that this is always in the victims' best interests. Considerable progress was made at the end of the 1970s, when there was at last an end to the judgement of victims from an ideological perspective. The dead were no longer good or bad, but victims deserving of compassion. This new perspective gave rise to the emergency ethic which has become increasingly prevalent. However, we were quick to forget that the values of the Cold War were combined with Realpolitik *and that moral outrage above all helped to counter totalitarian thinking.*

From Afghanistan to Angola, Nicaragua to Cambodia, not one major Western power used humanitarian aid as its sole arm against the Soviets, the Cubans or the Vietnamese: political or military action were key components in a strategy of containment in which humanitarian aid played but a minor role.

Nowadays, from Bosnia to Rwanda, the emergency ethic has rebounded on the victims. They are now seen in terms of their immediate suffering rather than as fellow human beings, citizens fighting for values or simply to stay alive, but — if fortunate enough to survive — hungry mouths to feed. Humanitarian aid was Europe's only real response to Serb aggression in Bosnia and this same response was proffered in Rwanda, when the genocide was over and it was too late. Here the massive deployment of humanitarian aid around Goma somehow disguised the culpable failure to come to the assistance of Tutsis in mortal danger. In Bosnia, humanitarian aid elevated to the status of official policy has, in the final analysis, encouraged and fostered aggression while bringing public opinion to accept both the fait accompli *of the stronger party and an "ethnic" reading of the conflict. The humanitarian brotherhood is playing an increasingly amnesiac role, preventing all political analysis of the situation, sustaining the impression that these supposedly tribal struggles defy comprehension.*

In dealing with countries in ongoing wars of a local nature, humanitarian aid has acquired a near-monopoly of morality and international action. It is this monopoly that we seek to denounce. Humanitarian action is noble when coupled with political action and justice. Without them, it is doomed to failure and, especially in the major crises covered by the media, becomes little more than a plaything of international politics, a conscience-salving gimmick. Unlike in the last decade, there is an enormous disparity today between the principles and values proclaimed by our societies on the one hand, and the measures taken to defend them on the other. We now endlessly commemorate past struggles against tyranny, congratulate ourselves on the mythical advance of justice and, at the same time, stand by idly when faced with the first indisputable genocide since the Second World War or the return of "ethnic cleansing" to the heart of Europe.

How can we think of passing food through the window while doing nothing to drive the murderer from the house, feeding hostages without attempting to confront their kidnapper, or, worse still, feeding the murderer after the crime. These are not humanitarian acts. Nevertheless, a purely humanitarian approach acts as a blindfold which allows us to bask permanently in the warmth of our own generosity. A perverse concept of humanitarian action may well triumph in the absence of policy and justice. It is far from certain that the victims are getting anything out of it. Humanitarian organisations which attach some importance to words and deeds will be facing unprecedented challenges in the years ahead.

I

Five crises

1

BURUNDI

O ften described as Rwanda's twin, in spite of all that separates them, Burundi has been in a state of crisis since autumn 1993, when the world was given a foretaste of what was to happen in Rwanda the following spring. The assassination of President Melchior Ndadaye by soldiers on 21 October 1993 triggered large-scale massacres and caused many to flee for their lives. Most estimates suggest that within weeks the massacres claimed 50,000 to 80,000 lives and drove almost 700,000 people to seek refuge in Rwanda, Tanzania and Zaire. In addition to the refugees, over 80 percent of whom have since returned to the country, the October crisis led to substantial population movements within Burundi itself. In August 1994, there were still about a quarter of a million displaced people in the capital, many of whom were sheltering in camps under the protection of the army, not daring to return to their hillsides. The Burundian crisis still smoulders, threatening to flare up at any moment. The failure to punish those responsible for the massacres, the constant insecurity, and the political instability after the murders of two successive presidents give cause for serious concern. The present uncertainty is exacerbated by the possible knock-on effects of the Rwandese crisis.

To an even greater extent than in Rwanda, massacres of unarmed people have been dismissed as ethnic clashes. Yet the genocide in Rwanda, far from overshadowing the killings in Burundi, makes plain the gravity of the racist syndrome in which both countries have been locked for the last thirty years.

◆

1965-72: The political and ethnic spiral

The political battles surrounding Burundi's independence in 1962 were fought by princely factions, and had nothing to do with rifts between Hutus and Tutsis. The nationalist victors of the 1961 elections, the Union for National Progress (UPRONA) drew its members from all circles. The ethnic virus was initially carried only by the educated, who were influenced by the Rwandese "social" revolution of 1959. This was seen by some Hutus as a model and by the Tutsis, marked by the arrival in Burundi of over 50,000 Rwandese refugees, as something to be avoided at all cost. The breaking point came in October 1965, when an attempted coup by high-ranking Hutu gendarmes was immediately followed by the massacre of several hundred Tutsi farmers in the midwest of the country. A lasting fear was instilled in the Tutsi community; the ensuing repression — which claimed several thousand lives — marked the beginning of a period in which Hutus were edged out of political life. Power was monopolized by the Tutsis, among whom a hard-line tendency, strongest in the south of the country, and especially the Bururi province, grew in strength.

Towards the end of April 1972, this sidelining of the Hutus had a result: the explosion in south-west Burundi of a Hutu rebellion in which several thousand Tutsis were slaughtered. The revolt was put down harshly and the authorities seized the chance to organize two months of widespread reprisals against Hutus who — by virtue of their education, activities or position — stood out from the crowd. This genocidal killing of the Hutu élite left the Tutsis with a monopoly on power, the army and the upper echelons of the administration. More important still, it led to the crystallization of a Hutu consciousness, rooted in the memory of these massacres (referred to as the *Ikiza* or "scourge") reputed to have claimed almost 100,000 lives, and sent nearly 300,000 refugees fleeing into neighbouring countries. The division of political life along ethnic lines was dictated primarily by a fear that pervaded all areas of society, and by the vindictive hatred cultivated by hard-liners attributing extermination plans to the other ethnic group. It is in this vicious circle of vengeance and mutual fear, sustained by successive crises, that the separate Tutsi and Hutu identities are rooted — with the Tutsis looking back to 1965 and the Hutus to 1972.

The abolition of the monarchy in 1966 was followed by a series of *coups d'état*, in 1966, 1976 and 1987, which brought to power Tutsi soldiers from the south. As in Rwanda, the ethnicization of power was also coloured by regional or clan interests. The dictatorship of Colonel Michel Micombero, in which there was absolutely no power-sharing, gave way to President Bagaza's Second Republic. That regime was characterised by an effort to rebuild national unity on the twin foundations of social and economic development, to be paid for by rising coffee prices, and of ideology, involving the strengthening of the country's institutions and administration within an authoritarian single-party framework, the single party being UPRONA.

Some refugees returned, and Hutus were once again allowed access to secondary and university education, though this was not accompanied by any real political change. Only about 20 percent of the government and legislature were Hutus, even though they accounted for 85 percent of the population as a whole. Worse still, government repression steadily intensified in the 1980s, with anti-clerical measures bringing the state into conflict with the church. This political deadlock was exploited by the Hutu refugees in Europe, Rwanda and Tanzania, who founded the Hutu People's Liberation Party (PALIPEHUTU) in 1980. Ethnically chauvinist, this party decried the "Tutsi apartheid" and harped on about the danger of a repetition of 1972. It called for democracy based on the Rwandese model, i.e. rule by the majority, with itself as the natural representative of 85 percent of the population. The 1980s saw mounting tit-for-tat violence. The ruling Tutsi minority became obsessed by security, while the Hutus proclaimed an imminent rerun of the 1972 massacres. The coup of September 1987, which brought Pierre Buyoya to power, opened a new period, marked by a degree of liberalization and an end to actions against the church, but also by the burden of the past and the memory of the massacres.

1988-93: hope of national reconciliation

Rumours and tracts spread by PALIPEHUTU and Tutsi extremists led, on 15 August 1988, to an eruption of violence in the Ntega and Marangara districts of north-east Burundi. Under the influence of alarmist propaganda centred on the threat of a repeat of 1972, Hutu farmers were incited to murder their Tutsi neighbours in a pre-emptive strike. This strategy of the self-fulfilling prophecy, which engenders violence by stimulating the fear of violence, led to massacres which, following a tragically familiar scenario, were immediately followed by bloody reprisals by the armed forces.

This new tragedy, which claimed 5,000 to 10,000 lives and created 50,000 refugees, refreshed memories of 1965 and 1972. It revived the Tutsis' fears, traumatizing a new generation of Hutus and foreshadowing the massacres of 1993. The crisis also revealed the potential for violence of a society with a significant proportion of young people living in rural areas, barely scraping out an existence on tiny farms, with no prospects, and where, as in neighbouring Rwanda, rapid population growth and the scarcity of land play a crucial role in exacerbating tensions.

Just as Burundi seemed about to erupt into civil war, President Pierre Buyoya surprised everyone by launching a policy of liberalization. In October 1988, after forming a government representing both ethnic groups and led by a Hutu, he set up a joint committee to study the issue of national unity and draft a Charter condemning exclusion and discrimination between Hutus and Tutsis for adoption by referendum in February 1991. Refugees from 1988 returned en masse at the end of the year, while those from previous exoduses started coming home at the end of 1990. Political prisoners were released in 1989 and 1990. Freedom of speech was recognized, two human rights organisations were set up, and in March 1992, a democratic constitution was adopted. Political parties were formed: the main opposition grouping — the Front for Democracy in Burundi (FRODEBU) — which had been set up clandestinely in 1986 by returnees from Rwanda, was legalized in July. A new political culture of non-violent confrontation and power-sharing seemed about to be born.

However, ethnic extremism was deep rooted and thrived in the climate of tension fostered by the outbreak of civil war in Rwanda. In 1991 the racist magazine *Kangura* began inciting PALIPEHUTU to take up arms. Following the death of its leader in August 1990 in Tanzania, PALIPEHUTU had won the backing of the Habyarimana regime in Rwanda. Extremists launched armed attacks in southern Burundi in August 1990, and in late November 1991 Bujumbura and the north-eastern province of Cibitoke were attacked with the aim of derailing the reforms under way. This crisis and the ensuing repression claimed a thousand more lives. Similarly, coup attempts by Tutsi political and military extremists were thwarted in March 1989 and March 1992. The continuation of the violence in spite of the intensive dialogue built up over three years, the spread of civil disobedience by Hutu radicals — rejection of the courts and forces of law and non-payment of taxes — and the alarmist rumours alluding to 1972 maintained an unhealthy climate in the run-up to the deadlines for democratization.

Notwithstanding an election campaign marked by a resurgence of sweeping ethnic generalizations, the transition to democracy in June 1993 was almost exemplary. The FRODEBU candidate, Ndadaye, defeated Buyoya, winning 64 percent of the vote, and his party carried 80 percent of the seats in the national assembly. Tutsi-dominated UPRONA now found itself in opposition. The election of a Hutu president was a spectacular turnaround, although it is inaccurate to put everything down to the ethnic divide, since two thirds of UPRONA's deputies were also Hutus. The new president stressed his national role, denouncing the "cult of tribalism" as a disease and forming a government headed by a woman close to UPRONA. The new authorities even seemed to have found a *modus vivendi* with the overwhelmingly Tutsi army, whose loyalty appeared to be confirmed when it foiled an attempted coup in early July.

October–November 1993: from coup to massacre

Three months later the change of government appeared to have been accepted as a fact of life. This was in spite of the tensions caused by the appointment of new FRODEBU administrators at all levels of the provincial authorities, by the wave of transfers in the school system, the multiplication of land disputes as a result of the return of refugees to an overpopulated country and plans to restructure the army. But all this was turned upside down by the coup attempt carried out on the night of 20 October to 21 October by a Bujumbura-based army battalion. The presidential palace was surrounded and President Ndadaye murdered along with some of his aides. Despite this disastrous blow to the government, the rebels failed to find any real support from the army or civilians and two days later they lost their nerve and fled to Zaire.

The damage, however, was irreparable. The death of the first elected president, who embodied democratic change and had become — even in the eyes of the opposition — the guardian of national unity, immediately unleashed the most violent emotions and extremist programmes. A racist frenzy that set Hutus and Tutsis at each others' throats exploded with the precision of a time bomb on 21 October, becoming still more violent the following day when the president's death was announced by Hutu extremist radio stations in Rwanda.

The massacres of late October cannot be explained away as the consequences of the coup. There was another dimension to the tragedy, which was connected to the coup but invested with a logic all of its own. Observers have drawn parallels between the killings in Burundi and the Rwandese genocide. In both cases, the wrath of the people was used to justify unspeakable acts. In both cases, fear was manipulated by the systematic use of racist propaganda and malicious rumour in order to drive an entire society into a murderous frenzy. False reports of massacres were used to provoke real ones and people were incited to kill or be killed. The scale of the carnage can be seen from the figures — 50,000 to 80,000 dead in just a few weeks — and the innumerable eyewitness accounts of the massacres which, from 21 October, drenched the hills of northern, eastern and central Burundi with blood. This organized terror merits the description of "rural pogroms", with all that the term implies in the way of systematic slaughter and the complicity of the local authorities in at least forty districts of the country.

Pogroms in the hills

The process followed the same pattern each time. Bridges were destroyed and trees felled to block the roads; ropes and jerry cans of petrol were handed out to gangs of young militants armed with machetes, who started arresting people and rounding them up in commercial outlets or public buildings. This time the victims were the Tutsis and Hutu militants from the UPRONA opposition party. Ethnic selection also took place in schools. In Kibimba, almost a hundred Tutsi pupils were burned alive in a disused shop, which was first padlocked and then torched. In the ensuing days, the Rwandese radio stations broadcast appeals for the people to resist and aired unfounded reports of massacres of civilians carried out by the army in the north (Kayanza, Busiga and Muyinga) — not to mention incitations to murder put out by *Radiotélévision des Mille Collines* (RTLM). The hunt was on for Tutsis and their Hutu "accomplices".

No one was safe, boys and men were arrested, hacked to death, their homes burned down and entire families (women, children, the elderly and the sick) slaughtered on the spot. Teachers and civil servants were herded into village halls and massacred (in Butezi, for instance, they were burned alive). With the help of local gangs, teachers organized the murders of their colleagues and pupils, as in Giheta or Rusengo. Gangs of killers, summoned by drums or whistles, travelled by van from the areas where the killing was most advanced to those areas where the "work" had yet to be accomplished. Doctors were massacred with their patients at hospitals (Mutaho, Ntita, etc.) and there was no respect for the

BURUNDI: THE MASSACRES AND THE FLIGHT OF REFUGEES AT THE END OF 1993

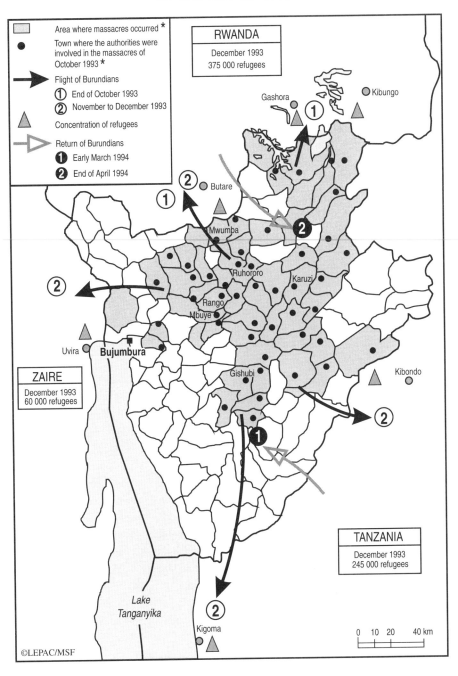

Sources: MSF; HCR; KOMERA.

* Provisional map based on information available in February 1994.

sanctuary of convents or parish halls. Priests were killed. Corpses were thrown into cesspits, into rivers, or dumped by the road-sides or in front of their houses.

These pogroms hit entire provinces (Karuzi, Kirundo, rural Bujumbura) and entire districts, including Rango, Ruhororo or Mwumba (in the north), Gishubi or Mbuye (in the centre), were ethnically cleansed. Many people were implicated in these pogroms, among them members of FRODEBU or allied parties only recently appointed by the new government, district administrators, school principals or civil servants.

The army reacted to these massacres in a variety of ways. In the first few days, the army and the gendarmerie were paralysed, seemingly unable to prevent the frenzied slaughter, only turning up a couple of days later to pick up survivors. In some cases these rescue missions stumbled upon organized gangs in the act of committing a massacre, leading to skirmishes and further loss of life. Then, particularly in the south, indiscriminate and systematic reprisals were carried out against Hutu farmers, resulting in large-scale massacres. The inconsistent orders issued by the government, the failure to punish the culprits, the despair and clamour of the survivors and the displaced brought, in November and December, a flurry of revenge attacks involving soldiers.

Mass exodus

The Burundian crisis caused large-scale population movements both inside the country and across its borders. People fled in waves. In the first few days of the massacres, almost 300,000 Hutus fled to Rwanda, most of them women and children fleeing in anticipation of army massacres. Then, in the weeks after, another 400,000 people fled to Rwanda, Tanzania and Zaire, ending up in overcrowded camps ravaged by hunger and dysentery.

The international response to this flood of refugees reflected the general lack of interest in the Burundian crisis. The international community was slow to help and had great difficulty distributing enough food aid to keep the refugees alive. In December 1993, Burundian refugees in the camps of Burenge and Nzangwa were still suffering malnutrition when warehouses a small distance away were full of food. It was to be some time before the funding, co-ordination and organizational problems were resolved, and it would take three months — and many thousands of deaths — before the camps were adequately supplied. By early March 1994, most of the refugees in Tanzania had returned to Burundi, followed

Aid to refugees in Rwanda

◆

The massive exodus of 700,000 refugees to neighbouring countries highlighted serious defects in the organization of aid to refugees. Despite the rapid mobilization of many humanitarian organizations already in the region, the nutritional condition of the refugees deteriorated quickly. This malnutrition, compounded in most camps by a dysentery epidemic, caused a fivefold increase in normal mortality rates, and it was four months before relief organizations were able to stabilize the situation.

Malnutrition was caused by a number of factors. After establishing basic rations at a ridiculously low level, the World Food Programme (WFP) failed to provide a sufficiently regular supply of food aid. Furthermore, it took the International Federation of Red Cross Societies and the Rwandese Red Cross over three months to set up a reliable and fair food distribution system in the camps.

Delays in planning the camps, in switching the sites of some, providing sanitation and distributing soap and jerry cans prevented the timely application of the measures needed to contain diarrhoea and its spread. Overwhelmed by the scale of the task, the United Nations High Commission for Refugees (UNHCR) and Non-Governmental Organizations failed to react in time.

In addition to the delays and shortcomings that unfortunately typify the UN agencies in emergency situations, the financial constraints on the WFP and, to a lesser degree, the UNHCR also played their part in making matters worse. Without these financial problems, the two agencies would undoubtedly have been better able to plan their work, provide aid in good time and, more generally, demonstrate greater efficiency.

The Burundian crisis is a good example of the double talk and indifference of the international community in emergencies neglected by the media. With very few exceptions, the benefactors dragged their feet and released sufficient resources only when the plight of the refugees had become acute. Once again, their desire for publicity took precedence over the need for efficiency and the demands for emergency action.

in late April by almost 200,000 refugees fleeing the troubles caused by the Rwandese crisis. Within the country, almost 250,000 people (mainly Tutsis, but including Hutu members of UPRONA) were either sheltering in the capital, as they had since November, or in camps protected by the armed forces. The ongoing problem of displaced persons attests to the climate of uncertainty and insecurity that continues to reign in the countryside almost a year after the massacres of autumn 1993.

Late 1993-94: a looming crisis

Despite their scale, the massacres of late 1993 went largely unnoticed in the West. When not simply forgotten or ignored, the Burundian crisis was treated by the media in terms of "ethnic clashes" and a refugee problem. The media's discretion was undoubtedly due in part to the fact that most of the pogroms in Burundi took place in the hills, away from the gaze of the few journalists present in the country, most of whom rarely strayed from the main roads. But the international indifference has to be put down to the dominant stereotype of Africa as a continent in crisis, prone — through culture and climate — to atavistic violence and perpetual disaster. This caricature — which foreshadowed the indifference to the Rwandese genocide — has to a great extent pushed into the background the crucial issue of bringing to justice those responsible for the massacres. This is not only a moral issue, but a political one. The absence of international pressure and the lack of political will on the part of the Burundian authorities to apportion blame — for either the coup or the massacres — coupled with the inertia of the judiciary mean that the guilty go unpunished, poisoning the atmosphere and building up uncertainties for the future.

Since December 1993, the country's institutions have gradually resumed work under the auspices of the UN. But Burundi was knocked back into institutional limbo by the death of President Cyprien Ntaryamira, alongside his Rwandese counterpart, in the missile attack over Kigali on 6 April 1994. The atmosphere in Bujumbura became charged. Several districts of the city were ethnically cleansed, starting with Kamenge in the north and continuing into other parts of town in the early months of the year. The quest for a compromise between FRODEBU and the opposition, both dominated by hard-liners, has been punctuated by several "stay-at-home" strikes, which have rekindled the violence. In February and March 1994, FRODEBU extremists began arming their supporters, particularly in Kamenge. These militias were disarmed in late April with the consent of the interim president, Sylvestre Ntibantunganya, but arms remain in circulation and assassinations and acts of provocation or revenge are multiplying in the capital and the countryside. The influx of Rwandese refugees, including many former members of the militias that carried out the genocide, only makes matters worse, and extremists on all sides are trying to force the hand of their opponents. One year on from the 1993 crisis, Burundi is on the edge of the precipice.

At a time when preventive diplomacy is the flavour of the month in international circles, everything must be done to try and prevent another flare-up. The international community must move to isolate the extremists, defuse the propaganda and break the vicious circle of vengeance and fear. It is vital that something is done to end the impunity — a seedbed for new violence — enjoyed by those responsible for the massacres. The deployment of human rights observers, in Burundi and Rwanda alike, to investigate the massacres and reassure the population would be the most useful contribution the international community could make to the efforts of those Burundians who are striving to restore the rule of law and neutralize ethnic chauvinism.

Hutu and Tutsi: a false ethnic divide

◆

Massacres in Burundi and genocide in Rwanda have turned the spotlight on the antagonism between Hutus and Tutsis, and this has led most commentators to speak of ethnic conflict. But the two groups are not separated by history, language, religion or territory, nor even distinguished by the often cited physical traits — the short Hutu majority against the tall Tutsi minority. The ethnic divide is thus not attributable to cultural differences or natural atavism, it is a product of contemporary history.

An archaic social split. — Burundi and Rwanda were already proper nations before colonization, kingdoms moulded by 400 years of common culture and politics. Contrary to popular myth, the oral tradition has no stories of invasions that would explain the present conflicts. The history of population movements in the Great Lakes region is certainly complex but these movements date back two thousand years and do not help explain today's tragedy. The cultural integration of the countries goes back a long way: all Burundians and all Rwandese speak the same ancient Bantu language (Kirundi and Kinyarwanda respectively) without any differences of vocabulary or accent between different sections of the population.

The term *ubwooko* (category) designated, when applied to Hutu and Tutsi, a kind of super clan with distinct socio-economic features: the Tutsis raised livestock and the Hutus were farmers. In fact these two patrilineal social groups participated in the same farming/pastoral economy, intermarried and lived as neighbours. They lived side by side in a very densely populated region (around 200 inhabitants per square kilometre) — there have never been separate Hutu or Tutsi territories.

The division between Hutus and Tutsis hardened during power struggles. The political and social dominance of a Tutsi aristocracy forged by pastoral clienteles and princely marriages gained a firmer hold in both countries during the 18th century, but the label feudal does not fit: there were no Hutu serfs under Tutsi lords, only rich and poor in each group, both of which were the subjects of a sacrosanct monarchy.

The emergence of racism. — The picture changes in the colonial period (1890-1962) when this traditional society was caricatured and manipulated under the influence of Gobineau-style racial theories. Tutsis and Hutus were categorized as two different races: one a superior race of Hamitic invaders who had come from the Middle East via Ethiopia or Egypt, the second a subject race of Negro Bantus. Missionaries in the grip of pseudo-Biblical myths, who had a decisive ideological influence, saw the Tutsis as "Hamitic Semites" or "African Jews".

This racial cliché has been advanced as a catch-all explanation for all cultural, social and political questions in the two countries. In 1948, a Belgian doctor wrote: "The Hamites are 1.90m tall and slenderly built. They have straight noses, high foreheads and thin lips... They have a distant, reserved, courteous and elegant manner. Masked by a certain air of refinement one can glimpse cunning. The rest of the population is Bantu, the Bahutu. They are Negroes with all the Negroid characteristics: a flat nose, thick lips, low forehead and a brachycephalous skull. They are childish in nature, both timid and lazy, and as often as not, extremely dirty. They form the serf class..."

This racialization of society underpinned the implementation of colonial rule: the colonial administrators found that the Tutsis, who they saw as being born to rule, were their natural allies, and in the early 1930s all the Hutu chiefs — and there were many in Burundi — were relieved of their functions. The Tutsis were also favoured educationally and administratively, and by the eve of independence they had become the scapegoats for all the frustrations aroused by foreign rule.

At the time of independence in the early 1960s, Rwanda and Burundi were handed a poisoned chalice but the worst could still have been avoided. Unfortunately, the new élite also mouthed the clichés coined by the colonizers, and politics was soon dominated by an ethnic fundamentalism that fed a cycle of massacres. From then on, ethnic identification, with no cultural basis to it, fed and blossomed on the fear created by past or potential acts of violence. To be a Tutsi or a Hutu today means remembering who killed your parents 15 years ago and imagining who might kill your own child in 10 years time. Both Burundi and Rwanda are now caught in a vicious circle fuelled by ethnic politics.

2

RWANDA

*R*wanda, *a small East African country hitherto largely unknown in the West, has been headline news since spring 1994. The assassination of the Rwandese president, Juvénal Habyarimana, on 6 April triggered one of the greatest tragedies of the 20th century. In the space of less than three months, amid general indifference, between 500,000 and a million people were killed, victims of a systematic campaign of extermination. The international community looked on as the genocide of the Tutsis and their so-called accomplices continued, and it was not until the end of June that France decided to intervene, and the end of July before Western and African countries mobilized in response to the televised pictures of an entire people fleeing across the Zairian border. The genocide, first given the generic label of ethnic violence, then relegated to a simple side-effect of civil war, was finally blotted out by the humanitarian disaster of the Zairian refugee camps and subsumed into an undiscriminating catalogue of tit-for-tat massacres. The lack of reaction to this tragedy raises fundamental questions about the role of the international community and the role of humanitarian aid in political crises as we move towards the end of the century.*

◆

1959-89: from "social revolution"
to "democracy by quota"

Between 1959 and 1961, on the eve of Rwanda's independence, a so-called social revolution swept away the ancient Tutsi monarchy and led to the creation of a Hutu republic. However, the revolt of a small Hutu élite against the Tutsi élite protesting against the unequal treatment of the two groups by the colonizers, far from repairing the long-standing rifts in Rwandese society, only deepened them and reversed discrimination in favour of the Hutus. The propaganda of PARMEHUTU, the party which spearheaded the revolution with the support of the Catholic church and the Belgian administration, persistently focused on the division between the "Bantu Hutus" and the "Hamitic Tutsi colonisers".

This reversal of the feudal system led to the exclusion of Rwandese Tutsis from their own country, hundreds were assassinated in early November 1959 and 22,000 were forcibly deported to Bugesera in the east (at the time an insalubrious area). With Rwanda's independence in July 1962, 120,000 Tutsis had already fled a hostile country to take refuge in neighbouring states. An attempted revenge attack carried out at Christmas 1963 by exiles living in Burundi was followed by reprisals in early 1964 that left at least 10,000 Tutsis dead and eliminated their leadership. This in turn provoked a fresh exodus of 150,000 to 250,000 people.

Less than two years after independence over half the Tutsi population of Rwanda was in exile, and the issue of their return and resettlement was to poison Rwandese politics thereafter. Rwanda provides a tragic illustration of the consequences of an unresolved refugee problem: twenty-five years later the second generation of exiles would take up arms under the banner of the Rwandese Patriotic Front (RPF) and try to return by force. By 1990, these first African refugees formed a community some 600,000 strong, living mostly in Uganda, Burundi, Zaire and Tanzania, a diaspora scornfully dismissed as a handful of feudalists cast aside by a democratic revolution.

Within the country, ethnicity lay at the heart of the regime's ideology. A new wave of persecution provoked another exodus in early 1973 and paved the way for the coup engineered in July by General Juvénal Habyarimana. This brought to power a Hutu faction from the north-west (the Gisenyi and Ruhengeri prefectures) which considered itself to be the least tainted by Tutsi influence, and the new regime was to play the ethnic card to marginalize the Hutu élites of the centre and south. Ethnic origin was recorded on identity cards because it determined access to schools and jobs under a quota system that restricted the Tutsi share to 9 percent. The fact that the country's leaders belonged to the majority group was advanced as proof of the regime's democratic base, though it was simply a dictatorship. In 1988, Habyarimana, now presidential candidate of the country's single party, the National Revolutionary Movement for Development (MRND), was re-elected with 99 percent of the vote. Thus, he could claim to represent the majority, namely the Hutu population. In Burundi the Tutsi regime sought to justify itself on security grounds. In Rwanda the Hutu regime claimed to represent the majority. But in both cases military dictatorship and single parties were merely expressions of the monopoly of power by a minority mafia.

1989-94: rising hopes and tensions

As the 1980s drew to a close, the regime had to grapple with economic and social problems that put the spotlight on the contradiction between the official populist line and the political control exercised by a small mafia of army officers and businessmen, labelled *akazu* ("the household"). At the same time a new civil society of intellectuals and small entrepreneurs started to emerge. Associations sprang up and the press started to denounce government corruption and its promotion of ethnic strife as a way of legitimizing its hold on power. Despite arrests and trials, the movement gathered pace — in August 1990, 33 intellectuals published a manifesto calling for an end to obligatory membership of the single party.

Meanwhile, the fortunes of the Tutsi diaspora took a decisive turn in Uganda where about a third of the refugees lived. The Ugandan civil war of the 1980s affected them directly. In 1982, Milton Obote's regime launched a wave of violent persecution of the Rwandese refugees and about 45,000 of them were forced back into Rwanda, where they remained in camps for two years. In 1984, some of the Tutsi exiles joined Yoweri Museveni's guerilla army in western Uganda and by the time Uganda's National Resistance Army (NRA) came to power in 1986, they accounted for nearly 20 percent of its forces. The RPF was set up the following year: it called for the right of return and started developing new nationalist and progressive policies; very different from those pursued by the former monarchist leaders.

With the collusion of sympathizers within the Ugandan army and support from Hutu opponents of the regime who joined them from Rwanda, the RPF took the offensive on 1 October 1990 and marched into north-eastern Rwanda. The outbreak of fighting led to the intervention of Belgian and French forces to evacuate their nationals. But France's intervention, although presented as a humanitarian mission of protection, went beyond this. French troops took part in the fighting in support of the Rwandese Armed Forces and ensured the regime's survival by blocking the advance of the RPF's *inkotanyi* ("fighting men").

Under pressure from home and abroad, President Habyarimana was forced to make political concessions in June 1991. A dozen parties were formed and then, following widespread demonstrations, a coalition government embracing the opposition and the former single party was set up in April 1992. The RPF reorganized in the north under the military leadership of General Paul Kagame, while a Hutu, Alexis Kanyarengwe, was appointed as party president. After a raid on Ruhengeri in January 1991, during which many political prisoners were liberated, the Front advanced into the tea-growing area of Mulindi in the Byumba prefecture. In June 1992, contact was established between the RPF and the domestic opposition, a cease-fire was agreed, and negotiations opened between the government and the rebels in Arusha (Tanzania) in the presence of international observers. Agreements signed in 1992 and 1993 provided for the establishment of a power-sharing transitional government as talks continued to find a compromise on the military front.

Although concessions were made under international pressure, the civil war had brought to the surface a nakedly racist faction. In Kigali the president's supporters — consisting of the former single party, the MRND, and a more radical formation set up in March 1992, the Coalition for the Defence of the Republic (CDR) — started pumping out ethnic propaganda and calling for a common Hutu front against the exiles (referred to as *inyenzi*, "cockroaches"). The magazine *Kangura* ("Awakening") published an incessant diet of anti-Tutsi propaganda. "The ten Hutu commandments" published in December 1990 put forward a veritable programme of apartheid aimed at neutralizing "the enemy within" that threatened "the Bantu people". In November 1992 an MRND leader close to President Habyarimana made a speech near Gisenyi calling for the Tutsis to be thrown into the rivers and sent back to their supposed country of origin, Ethiopia — a sinister omen.

For three years the Tutsi community was the butt of provocation, violence and pogroms, the scapegoat for all abuses in periods of tension. When the civil war started it was labelled a "fifth column" by Hutu extremists. The massacres of Kibirira in October 1990, Bigogwe in January 1991 (extermination of a whole regional group of Tutsis), Bugesera in March 1992, Kibuye in October 1990 and Gisenyi in early 1993 left thousands of dead.

In March 1993 an international inquiry mounted by human rights organizations denounced those responsible for the killings, singling out the groups close to the president's family. Significantly, every time progress was made in the negotiations the extremist members of militias set up in 1992 by the MRND and the CDR — who became known as the *interahamwe* ("united attackers") and the *impuzamugambi* ("those who have a common purpose") — instigated a wave of violence on the pretext of fending off "Tutsi infiltrators". A year before the events of 1994, amid international indifference, all the ingredients for genocide were in place. France, in particular, which was the main bulwark of the regime, having equipped and trained its army, never took any clear position on this racial totalitarianism that threatened the entire peace and democratization process.

A fresh RPF offensive in February 1993 was again opposed by France, which stepped up its military presence. The following month negotiations resumed in Arusha and led to a decision to facilitate negotiations between the two sides by creating a buffer zone under the control of a group of neutral military observers dispatched by the Organization of African Unity. Fighting resumed, causing 900,000 people to flee, as much owing to the incitement of the routed Rwandese army as to fear of the RPF, a presage of what was to come the following year. Despite all this, the Arusha agreements, which became the country's constitutional charter, were signed on 4 August 1993 by the RPF and the coalition government. The French troops left in December, handing over to 2,500 soldiers of the UN Assistance Mission to Rwanda (UNAMIR).

In January 1994, however, the extremist faction acted to prevent the setting-up of the institutions provided for in the agreements. President Habyarimana took his oath of office but acts of violence (above all, the assassination of an opposition leader) blocked the Assembly and the formation of the transitional government. The opposition parties were insidiously provoked and manipulated by factions intent on playing the ethnic card and promoting "Hutu power". From the summer of 1993 the *interahamwe* and the *impuzamugambi* had been armed and trained by members of the presidential guard. A new radio, Radiotélévision libre des Mille

Collines (RTLM), financed and staffed by extremists close to President Habyarimana, poured out an unending stream of hatred directed at the Tutsis, democrats and all those involved in the Arusha agreements in general, who were described as traitors deserving punishment by "the people". The UN representative made no reaction to the mounting wave of violence in Kigali. On 5 April the UN Security Council renewed the UNAMIR's mandate. The next day the storm broke.

April-June 1994: assassination, the cue for genocide

On the evening of 6 April, the presidential plane was shot down as it was about to land in Kigali, killing President Habyarimana and his Burundian counterpart Cyprien Ntaryamira. Although the identities of the actual perpetrators remain a mystery, the president's death was clearly a signal. Within the hour, army blockades went up around Kigali, where the killings started the following morning. On 8 April, an interim government was formed with the backing of a group of officers known to be extremists. The new government's power base was from those close to the former president — MRND, CDR and the extremist partisans of Hutu power — and it explained away the carnage as a spontaneous explosion of "the people's anger".

But all the evidence points to an organized genocide: the death lists in circulation the day after the crash; the identity of the victims — some killed because of their origins (Tutsis), others because of their ideas (Hutu opponents of the regime or simply representatives of the kind of civil society that was anathema to the partisans of ethnic totalitarianism); the systematic nature of the massacres; the organized groupings to which the killers belonged — presidential guard, the *interahamwe* and *impuzamugambi* militias; the known connivance of many local authorities (prefects, mayors, elected representatives of the former single party, schoolteachers and policemen) which helped the militias track down and kill thousands of innocent victims accused of collaborating "with the enemy"; and finally the decisive role of Radio des Mille Collines, which called on its listeners to kill "even the children" and fill the common graves.

A look at the sequence of events shows that the motives for the genocide were political as well as racist. In Kigali, between 7 and 15 April, many prominent members of the Hutu opposition (the

RTLM, the radio of death

◆

"The grave is only half full. Who will help us fill it?" The messages broadcast by Radiotélévision libre des Mille Collines (RTLM) were unambiguous. On the day following the assassination of President Juvénal Habyarimana on 6 April 1994, it even broadcast the names and addresses of the "cockroaches" (Tutsis) and the "accomplices" (moderate Hutus) to be killed. In a few hours the *interahamwe* militia went to work with a transistor in one hand and a machete in another. The streets of Kigali filled with bodies, an eruption of violence that would soon spread throughout the country.

The RTLM was set up in August 1993 on the eve of the signing of the Arusha agreements with a clear objective in mind: to serve as the voice of a handful of Hutu extremists who feared the end of the Hutu monopoly of Radio Rwanda, which would henceforth have to be shared with the RPF. And they had support at the highest level: the funding came directly from the president's wife, Agathe Habyarimana, and Félicien Kabuga, whose daughter was married to one of the president's sons, Jean-Pierre Habyarimana. The ideologue of Hutu extremism, Ferdinand Nahimana took over the operation of the new station, the country's only private radio station, thanks to the support of the communications minister. A thought-provoking detail — to ensure power supplies in a crisis, the station's electricity was supplied directly by underground cable from the nearby presidential residence.

When the RPF bombed and partially destroyed the RTLM station on 17 April 1994 its journalists had no scruples about walking off with the national radio station's equipment to keep their own station on the air and also taking a mobile transmitter that would later enable them to go on broadcasting after the fall of Kigali. Radio des Mille Collines followed the retreating interim government, first to Butare and then Gisenyi. From around 7 July it was heard in Goma (Zaire) and then Cyangugu. By then it was inciting Rwandese not only to murder but also to flee en masse before the advancing RPF, thus contributing to the largest and most murderous bloodiest exodus in contemporary history. Trace of it was lost around 17 July, when it stopped broadcasting. In the meantime it had circulated in Zaire and in the safe haven controlled by French troops. Strangely, at a time when much is spoken about preventive diplomacy, no one appears to have thought that priority should have been given to putting this "radio of hate" out of action so that it could do no further harm.

prime minister of the coalition government, the president of the supreme court, members of the future transitional government, leaders of human rights associations, journalists, and so on) were killed for being traitors to the "Hutu race", while the Tutsis, from the most influential to the most humble, were victims of a nation-wide manhunt. The killings quickly spread to the north (Byumba and the Gisenyi area) and to the south towards the Burundian border, where the killings had the active support of Hutu refugees from Burundi. Between 10 and 22 April, the massacres spread to the prefectures of Kibungo, Cyangugu and Kibuye. They did not start in Butare until after the arrival of the presidential guard and the removal on 17 April of the prefect who had maintained order up until then. The killings continued until June in Kigali, Cyangugu and Kibuye. Civil servants and intellectuals, including priests, were certainly the prime targets but whole families of Tutsis or their Hutu "accomplices" were slaughtered, including the sick and the elderly, the wounded in ambulances and hospitals, women in maternity wards, children, and orphans.

The most frightening thing about this genocide — which was sophisticated in its organization if primitive in its means — is the seeming clear conscience of the thousands of people who set about the killings in response to deranged orders and the extreme cruelty that they inflicted on their victims: men and women burned or buried alive; hacked apart limb by limb and then decapitated; children bludgeoned to death; victims paying to be shot rather than be killed by machete; people who thought they had found refuge in the Cyangugu stadium, the Kabgayi camp or the Sainte Famille parish church in Kigali singled out, taken away and killed. At least thirty parish churches became slaughter houses where terrified crowds seeking sanctuary were attacked by grenades before being hacked to death by militiamen.

In less than three months, hundreds of thousands of people were slaughtered in one of the largest and most brutal massacres of modern times. The figures quoted — anywhere between 500,000 and a million dead — will probably never be verified but they serve to give an idea of the scale of the extermination campaign waged against a Tutsi community thought to number a little over a million before the massacres. But what allows us to qualify these massacres as genocide — as defined in the Convention on the Prevention and Punishment of Genocide, "acts committed with intent to destroy, in whole or in part, a national ethnic, racial or religious group" —

is the racist nature of the policy behind the killings and the openly declared desire to be rid of all Tutsis.

The international community: vacillation and inconsistency

Faced with an act of genocide without parallel since the defeat of Nazism, the international community was conspicuous by its inertia. This failure to act cannot be attributed to ignorance — the Rwandese crisis was amply covered by the media — nor to the lack of means — 2, 500 UN peacekeepers arrived in Kigali in December 1993. But the campaign of extermination continued for nearly three months without the slightest effort by the international community to put a stop to the carnage. And this feeling of impunity among the perpetrators encouraged them to go on killing on an unprecedented scale.

The first international reaction was to evacuate foreign nationals: France and Belgium, on 9 April, sent paratroopers in to save their citizens but a few days later they left, leaving the country in the hands of the killers. Very few Rwandese were saved by this operation, which was confined to foreign nationals. The killings continued under the very eyes of the intervention forces. The international community's second reaction was to reduce the number of Blue Helmets deployed in Kigali. The withdrawal of the Belgian troops, traumatized by the murder of ten of their soldiers guarding the assassinated prime minister, sapped the UN forces militarily and logistically, and they were then left practically powerless by the Security Council's decision to reduce their numbers from 2, 500 to 270.

Despite urgent appeals by the UN secretary general, Mr. Boutros Boutros-Ghali, the Security Council did not give its consent to an increase in the UN presence (UNAMIR II, 5,500 troops) nor to give it a mandate to protect the civilian population until 17 May. The United States, smarting from the Somalia débâcle, delayed the operation: as hundreds of thousands of Rwandese fell victim to an unprecedented campaign of terror, the US government put up endless financial and political obstacles to the actual deployment of the Blue Helmets. It took weeks of negotiation before the African countries that were willing to send troops to Rwanda received the necessary back-up and equipment. Even then their deployment was conditional on the conclusion of a cease-fire and the agreement of the parties involved, which amounted to giving the perpetrators of genocide the right of veto over protection of their victims by the international community.

This conception of the UN's intervention as a classic peacekeeping operation to keep two warring sides apart reflects the downplaying of the genocide and a shift of focus to the civil war, which resumed on 10 April and slowly but inexorably went the way of the RPF. Throughout the Rwandese crisis the genocide was de-dramatized by the use of clichés about "ethnic violence". Not until the visit of the UN High Commissioner for Human Rights to Kigali on 11 and 12 May and the special meeting of the human rights subcommittee in Geneva on 24 and 25 May was the word genocide pronounced in an international context. The Security Council's resolution of 17 May speaks coyly of an "exceptional situation" and "acts of genocide that may have been committed". The US administration forbade its spokespersons to use the term genocide for fear of encouraging public pressure for action and so having to assume its obligations as a signatory to the 1948 Convention.

So the international community stood by and watched the first genocide ever to be transmitted live on television. Ten weeks — and hundreds of thousands deaths — later, France decided *in extremis* to intervene in a country that had become a cross between a slaughter house and a giant refugee camp. On 22 June the Security Council authorized "Operation Turquoise", which started immediately but was rather overtaken by events as the RPF took Butare and Kigali on 3 and 4 July. In view of the massive population movements caused by the fighting and the propaganda still being pumped out by Radio des Mille Collines, the French decided to create a "safe area" in the south-west. While the creation of this area saved a few thousand lives and helped stabilize population movements within Rwanda, it also gave shelter to the militias and perpetrators of the massacres, who, in the absence of any real will to pursue those responsible for the genocide, remained in control and continued their propaganda campaign.

April-August 1994: massive population movements

On 17 July, the fall of Ruhengeri, followed by Gisenyi, provoked an exodus from the north-west on an unprecedented scale. In a few days nearly 800,000 people fled to the Goma region of Zaire. This massive movement of refugees, like the flight to Tanzania at the end of April, was fuelled by a mixture of fear of the RPF and

RWANDA, APRIL-AUGUST 1994: POPULATION MOVEMENTS

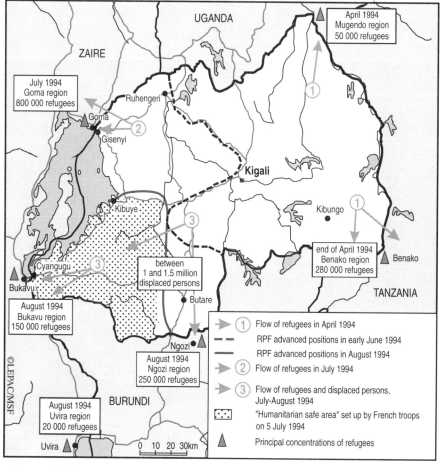

Source: MSF.

the propaganda of a government which, having encouraged a frenzied population to kill, now led its terrified followers into exile.

The sudden arrival of this human tide brought disaster. Cholera spread rapidly among people with no access to clean drinking water and who were living in cramped conditions. Humanitarian organizations were soon overwhelmed by the sheer scale of the exodus and the Goma camps, shown on television sets around the world, came to epitomize the Rwandese tragedy and block out the horror of the genocide. Western countries that had held back from carrying out preventive measures to stop the genocide, competed to aid the refugees, mounting one of the biggest relief operations ever. However, the deployment of huge logistic resources with massive media exposure was not enough to cope with the urgent needs of this human tide; the situation did not stabilize until a few weeks later and even then remained precarious. The cholera epidemic was gradually brought under control by August 1994 but dysentery and malnutrition are still rife in these over-crowded camps that are dependent on international aid.

The humanitarian trap

Quite aside from the problem of aid for the refugees, these population movements are a major element of the crisis and a threat to the country's future. At the end of August 1994, nearly a third of the population was still displaced or in refugee camps, crops were rotting in the fields and the new government, installed on 19 July in Kigali, ruled over a largely empty country. The crisis can be solved only by the return of the refugees but this is hampered by the climate of insecurity within the country and the power structure within the camps, where perpetrators of the genocide exert total control over the refugees.

The situation in Rwanda is far from being propitious to the return of displaced persons and refugees. Inquiries carried out in September and October 1994 by human rights organizations found evidence of wide-scale exactions and killings by RPF soldiers among the Hutu population. Apart from the difficulty an indigent government might have in controlling a powerful army sorely tempted to carry out reprisals for the massacres, the international community is slow to provide Rwanda with assistance needed for national reconstruction. The new regime is finding it difficult to normalise the situation inside the country when the state coffers are empty, the administration virtually non-existent and the army unpaid. Having allowed the genocide to take place in spring 1994, the international community appeared to be using the revenge killings of the RPF as a pretext for putting the killers and victims on an equal footing, thereby trivialising the genocide. The UN has dragged its feet in sending the international observers called for by the special rapporteur of the UN Human Rights Commission and agreed to by the new government. Nor has it shown any commitment, beyond declarations of intent, to pursue and bring to justice those responsible for the genocide, though this would be the best support the international community could provide for the sensitive process of national reconciliation and political renewal that Rwanda needs. This process will be so difficult that it places a

Benako, a humanitarian haven

◆

At the beginning of 1994 this place was still nameless. Two months later Benako had become the second largest town in Tanzania. What was a mere watering hole 30 kilometres from the Rwandese border is now home to over 200,000 refugees. At the end of April thousands of Rwandese fleeing the advance of the RPF in eastern Rwanda flooded over the border into Tanzania. Rapidly, however, it became clear that this massive exodus was anything but spontaneous, having been provoked by the exactions of the Rwandese Patriotic Front (RPF) and propaganda put out by the leaders of the Coalition for the Defence of the Republic (CDR) and the National Revolutionary Movement for Development (MRND) who played on the fears of the people to encourage large numbers to accompany them into exile, leaving the RPF to govern "the bush and the animals".

In just a few days a miniature Rwanda was reassembled on the other side of the border; the camp had the same model of administration (prefectures, communes, sections, etc.) and was governed by the former Rwandese authorities (prefects, mayors and militias). On arriving at Benako, the refugees were directed to their section of their commune of origin and registered by their leaders, who drew up lists for the distribution of food. The former authorities thus became the relief organizations' main interlocutor and took on a key role in aid distribution. Although the camp numbers were blatantly inflated, it took the United Nations High Commissioner for Refugees (UNHCR) months to recalculate them and revise downwards the quantity of aid distributed, part of which was siphoned off by the former Rwandese authorities.

By using aid as an instrument of coercion and a means of bankrolling their plans for revenge, the former authorities have gained total control of the camp. Benako is certainly a model camp with a semblance of perfect order and organization but the refugees live in a climate of threats and intimidation: the camp hospitals are having to treat injuries, bodies are found each morning, refugees sometimes ask to be transferred to other sites, mob lynchings take place, etc. The camps are in the hands of the killers. The relief organizations are aware of the problem but, when they tried to sideline these leaders, were attacked and had to evacuate the camp briefly in mid-June. Since then, in view of the weak response from the Tanzanian authorities and a lack of commitment by the Western powers, the UNHCR has actually recruited security guards proposed by camp leaders who are known to be responsible for the genocide. The refugees are being used as hostages, serving merely as a human reservoir and an economic base. They have become the pawns of the former Rwandese government.

question mark over the future of democracy in a country so divided that a good proportion of the population, under the influence of the former authorities, prefers to stay put on the other side of the border. In these circumstances one must ask whether the RPF, which has a very small constituency, is really anxious to encourage the return of an overwhelmingly hostile Hutu population. Whatever the case, the insecurity reigning in the country has led the UNHCR and most relief organizations to stop encouraging the return of the refugees.

The impasse is made total by the pressure and propaganda that the refugees are subjected to by the former authorities, which are blocking all attempts to return. The refugee camps in Tanzania and Zaire are controlled by those who instigated the genocide. Despite the international presence, threats and violence are the order of the day, and the authority of the UNHCR is regularly flouted by the criminals who run the camps.

The former authorities exert tight control over the refugees and play a pivotal role in the distribution of aid. In order to operate, international organizations have to deal with the camp leaders at the risk of recognizing and strengthening the control of those responsible for the genocide. They are, once again, faced with a long-standing humanitarian dilemma — should they feed the victims at the risk of giving the killers new strength. The problem is compounded by aid being used by these leaders to strengthen their grip on the refugees and diverted with a view to preparing their return to power in Rwanda. This manipulation of aid was first seen in the Tanzanian camps in May and goes on to a variable extent in all the camps. It is particularly widespread in the Goma camps where it has reached unprecedented levels. This manipulation of the status of camps as "humanitarian havens" for these purposes is not confined to Rwanda; in many countries refugee camps are used as bases for reconquest or destabilization and become a factor in perpetuating conflicts. But the scale of this phenomenon in Rwanda is unusual because of the size of the exodus, its organized nature and, above all, the genocide that preceded it. The situation is all the more worrying as the Rwandese crisis is far from over. Despite its military defeat, the former regime has not given up. Benefiting from a "demographic" legitimacy, it aspires to eventual military victory and the definitive decimation of the Tutsi community.

For these reasons the refugee problem cannot be managed on a purely humanitarian basis without playing into the hands of the extremists and prolonging the crisis. In that respect, it is essential that refugee assistance be controlled, that the camp leaders who were responsible for the genocide be separated from the main body of refugees and that human rights observers be deployed inside Rwanda. In the absence of a credible UNAMIR, The UNHCR and humanitarian organizations will have to keep a cool head and show determination to give the refugees real protection, prevent aid being siphoned off and create a climate in which massacres cannot take place.

3

ZAIRE

In a continent in the throes of change, Zaire is a textbook example of how an economy can stagnate, the state fall apart, and the country erupt. This vast land is bankrupt, ruined by thirty years of repression, rapacity and corruption. Economic decline has taken its toll on the average Zairian, who has slowly slipped from poverty into destitution, and the repeated failure to change the system has increased the risk of the country erupting into violence. While this hidden crisis has not yet led to civil war on the scale of Rwanda, Liberia or Somalia, the political stalemate has raised the temperature in regions which have long been prey to separatist temptations. In Shaba, for instance, people from Kasai have been subjected to what amounts to "ethnic cleansing", and in Kivu tensions between ethnic Rwandese and the indigenous population, which led to violent clashes in 1993, were exacerbated by the flood of refugees arriving from Rwanda from the summer of 1994 onwards.

◆

From independence to insolvency

The crisis in Zaire has been brewing since the country's independence when, on 30 June 1960, its Belgian colonial rulers departed. Zaire, then known as the Congo, entered a difficult period marked by political assassinations, Marxist-inspired revolts and separatist rebellion. The secession of Katanga on 11 July 1960 prompted the UN to intervene with a peacekeeping force which stayed for four years and was involved in the struggle to keep the country in one piece and the attempts to find a solution to the conflict. In 1965, a coup d'état enabled General Mobutu Sese Seko, as he became known, to come to power, imposing a dictatorship backed by ruthless repression and a one-party system.

In the early 1970s, the nationalization of the mining companies, a slump in the price of copper, the country's main resource, and sharply rising oil prices brought on the country's first serious economic difficulties. However, Zaire's immense mineral wealth, and international aid, provided a regular supply of hard currency which helped to hide the fact that its industrial base was crumbling away. From 1973 to 1978, foreign aid financed a string of white elephants which provided lucrative commissions for the regime's supporters. However, the biggest financial irregularities occurred just as the debt on these wasteful projects had to be paid off. The 1980s marked the highest point in the rise of Zaire's notorious "kleptocracy", which had been attacked in 1978 by the master of the art himself, Mobutu. In a famous speech on the "Zairian disease", the general fulminated against corruption and "upside-down values". This expression was to be used against him by his opponents twelve years later at the National Conference.

From 1982 onwards, legalized looting of the state coffers went on systematically, with all kinds of schemes being used to siphon off revenues from industry, in particular from Gécamines, the company which controlled Shaba's vast mineral resources and accounted for the bulk of the country's export earnings. From 1987 to 1988, 300 to 400 million dollars, almost a quarter of the state's annual revenue, disappeared into thin air; between 1984 and 1990, according to some estimates, over a billion dollars went missing from the Treasury.

In this murky atmosphere, the collapse of the mining industry was the clearest sign of bankruptcy. In the space of four years, copper output at Gécamines, which provided 70 percent of state revenue in its heyday, fell from 470,000 tonnes to 40,000 tonnes for lack of maintenance. As from the end of 1991, it did not pay the state a penny in tax or royalties, while public spending continued to mount. The only alternative left to the six successive governments in power in the period of the so-called "transition to democracy" was to print more money, thereby derailing what was left of the economy. Today, the state depends on diamond exports for its tax revenue, although over half of all diamonds are smuggled out of the country.

Zaire's hard times

In 1991, the dam burst and the country was plunged into anarchy reminiscent of the civil war years of 1960-65. Riots and looting in December 1990, September 1991 and January 1993 practically wiped out commercial and industrial investment in the capital and the main provincial towns. The looting, started by poverty-stricken soldiers, and then taken up by the urban poor, was the most tangible sign yet that the official economy had collapsed. The so-called informal economy has become the primary cash nexus, but in the prevailing anarchy, even the Zairians' fabled capacity for resourcefulness is no longer enough to keep their heads above water.

The following figures provide a graphic illustration of the deprivation the Zairians face: in November 1991, 5.2 percent of Kinshasa's inhabitants were suffering from malnutrition, 1 percent of them severely. By March 1994, the figures had risen to 10.7 percent and 2.5 percent respectively. There are currently some 80,000 children suffering from malnutrition in the capital, of whom 20,000 are severely malnourished, with the situation deteriorating all the time. Transport problems have seriously disrupted supplies to Kinshasa, causing prices of staple goods to soar. In the markets, sugar is now sold by the spoonful, bread by the slice, and the average poor urban-dwelling Zairian often cannot afford more than one meal a day. The problem is not confined to those at the bottom of the heap: some 300,000 to 500,000 civil servants, including armed forces personnel, have been hit by the crisis. In the last two years their salaries have been cut by inflation running at 2,000 to 3,000 percent a year.

One consequence of this situation is that throughout Zaire the health services have declined drastically. Less than half of all health and hospital facilities are operational and those still running are in a poor state, with few or no medical supplies. Poorly paid and unsupported health-workers feeling that they have been abandoned by a state that is going broke resign. The field is left open to a host of charlatans and patients are forced to pay exorbitant sums for treatment on the "free market". As a result, major endemic diseases are spreading rapidly — sleeping sickness, tuberculosis, cholera and even bubonic plague have all reappeared, even in the better-off areas such as Bandundu, which supplies Kinshasa with food. Preventive measures and screening programmes have been denied funding. AIDS is now one of the primary causes of death in the capital, and the number of HIV-positive people is estimated at 310,000, with some 30,000 people suffering from the disease who often receive no medical treatment.

The failure to open up the political system

The problems are exacerbated by the fact that international aid has been cut off following decades of embezzlement. After four years of difficult relations with international financial institutions, Zaire had its right to vote in the International Monetary Fund (IMF) taken away in May 1994, as a prelude to being excluded from the Fund altogether. Bilateral aid, which once pumped almost a billion dollars a year into the state coffers, dried up in 1992 and now Zaire's traditional patrons — Belgium, France and the United States — are left wondering as to how they can maintain diplomatic relations with a state that has practically ceased to exist. Aid donors and other international financial authorities would doubtless be more conciliatory if human rights were at last recognised and democratization was taking place. But that has not happened. Zaire is one country in sub-Saharan Africa whose National Conference, which brings together all the political parties with the purpose of reforming the system, has patently failed in this task and has lost much of its credibility as a result.

International pressures for political reform have ultimately had very little impact on General Mobutu, shielded in his palaces at Gbadolite and Kawele. He has elevated himself to the role of inaccessible monarch, deigning from time to time to referee in the factional squabbles of his fawning courtiers. Having agreed in October 1990 to the introduction of a multi-party system as of 1991, Mobutu refused to become involved in the work of the National Conference, which he had always despised, disclaimed wrong-doing which he had in fact encouraged, and distanced himself from the system of courtiers which he presided over. This isolation was not new; it started in the early 1980s. Having lost interest in the economy, except for the revenue it brought him, the president of Zaire is content to oversee petty arbitration, that is, when he is not playing the role of absentee landlord. Only two subjects are still important to him. First, his personal security, which has been ensured since the early 1980s by a special presidential guard set up with the help of Israeli advisers. Second, international affairs, in which he poses as the "wise man of Africa", mediating in his neighbours' battles (Angola, Rwanda, Burundi). From this perspective, the Rwandese crisis and the tide of refugees which arrived in Goma in July 1994 undoubtedly enabled him to break out of his isolation and re-emerge as someone the West has to deal with.

Launched in 1991, the so-called "sovereign" National Conference rapidly degenerated into pandemonium. The opposition, split into a myriad of political parties, rapidly disintegrated with the rise of regionalism. The political failure of the transition to democracy runs much deeper than the events of the last three years. "Democratization from the top down" has been paralysed partly by the lack of a clear distinction between the opposition and the traditional *nomenklatura*, and partly by the machinations of a political class which puts money and power before its much-touted concern for the well-being of the people. Money is the key to Zaire's political stalemate: the National Conference, the National Executive Council, the transitional parliament, the ministries, and so on, are still being used to earn big money in the old-fashioned way. Zaire's "new" political class threatens to re-group around institutions which are essentially there to redistribute bribes.

Some have expressed the hope that political reform will grow out of the "civil society" about which so much is made these days. Unfortunately, apart from a few development organizations which predate the transition and are mainly based around Kivu, Zairian civil society has not really gained its independence from the politicians. Of the thousands of organizations which claimed to represent civil society when the National Conference got under way, many were set up only to enable their representatives to draw the daily allowances granted to conference delegates, while others allowed themselves to be bought by the president's supporters. Over the months, the representatives of Zairian civil society have merely played a walk-on role, when not simply propping up other political groups and platforms, and they have gradually become estranged from their supporters.

Since late 1990, the weakness of the state and the failure of political reform have been matched by a strong rise in separatist tendencies in a country which has long been susceptible to breakaway movements. This resurgence of regionalism has been marked by fierce tensions in some areas, which have sometimes led to serious attempts at ethnic cleansing. The trouble spots have, however, been fewer than might have been expected in view of the way the economy has collapsed. The two regions which have seen the worst clashes between indigenous and non-indigenous people (*originaires* and *non-originaires*, as they are known in Zaire) are Shaba and Kivu. Both cases involved regional or ethnic conflicts that date back to the time of independence.

Ethnic cleansing in Shaba

In Shaba, renamed Katanga by the regional authorities, old ethnic/regional tensions have been reawakened with moves to weaken central government control. Katanga's secession from Zaire in 1960 was notable for its persecution of non-indigenous people, especially members of the Luba diaspora, some of them from the province of Kasai. They came to Shaba to work in the mines under colonial rule, and gradually worked their way up the ladder into some of the most sought-after jobs in the Union minière du Haut-Katanga (UMHK), the colonial administration and business. This persecution led to vicious "anti-Kasaian" pogroms and to the creation of concentration camps by the secessionist administration of Moise Tshombe, the president of Conakat, an association of "true" Katangans opposed to "the political and economic domination of Kasaian immigrants". On coming to power, President Mobutu, to prevent any resurgence of separatism, deliberately filled senior posts in Gécamines, the regional administrations and local army garrisons with Kasaians, especially Luba. This policy was reversed in September 1991 with the appointment of Kyungu wa Kumwanza, a Katangan, as the new governor of Shaba who immediately adopted measures discriminating against *non-originaires*. This xenophobic policy was well received because mining in Shaba has reached its lowest ebb ever as a result of the collapse of Gécamines, which had been bled dry to pay for the state's and the politicians' fiascos. The new regional authorities successfully turned the impoverished population's anger against the "carpetbagging" Kasaians.

The mines, teeming with rumours of massive lay-offs, were the scene of the worst attacks on the Kasaians. When a Luba from Kasai, Etienne Tshisekedi, was appointed Zaire's transitional prime minister in August 1992, the Katangans went on the rampage. Egged on by the governor, who declared that the Kasaians should be driven out "like insects", his followers were quoted on the radio as saying that they would "smear grease all over the Kasaians and slide them down the railway track back where they came from". Local papers, which had been used by Mobutu's propaganda machine, complained of the "incurable wound" represented by the Kasaians' presence and, backed by a number of local politicians, demanded independence for Katanga. In this frenzy of regionalist fervour, some Catholic priests went so far as to talk of a "Katangan liberation theology" in their sermons and young people, left to their own devices, without schools, jobs, or a future, were drawn into the hunt for Luba "colonists".

The troubles began in Likasi, in September 1992, when members of UFERI (the party of former Prime Minister Nguza Karl-I-Bond and Governor Kyungu) attacked, ransacked and burned the homes of Kasaians in the towns and on Gécamines housing estates. In panic, the Kasaians took refuge in military camps where they were protected by the Kasaian garrisons; in schools and churches where the clergy protected them; and in railway stations where they were to wait weeks for trains to take them to Kasai. Many of those driven out, lacking any money to pay for the trip, only survived because the authorities chartered dozens of trains and, even more crucially, the response from missionaries, the Red Cross and foreign humanitarian organizations was swift and effective. By June 1993, some 75,000 people had fled their homes in Likasi and were living in extremely precarious conditions in improvised camps, waiting to leave for a notional "ancestral homeland". Most of the camps were short of water, food, shelter, medical care, etc., and the mortality rate for children under five years-old was very high — twelve to twenty times higher than in the surrounding population, with six to ten deaths per 10,000 children per day.

By December 1992, 32,000 people had left Shaba, and the exodus continued unabated in the months that followed. By September 1993, almost 400,000 people had been driven back to Kasai and 135,000 displaced persons were camped in Shaba's railway stations, waiting to leave. By August 1994, two years after the start of the troubles, the number of people driven out was put at 700,000, and resettlement was causing problems. The outcasts arrived in Kasai, having lost everything, in transit camps where malnutrition was rife. Some surveys put the level of malnutrition and the mortality rate at four to six times higher than the figure for the communities taking them in. The displaced persons, who were mostly city-dwellers and had completely lost contact with their "region of origin", now found themselves struggling to survive either in an anarchic urban environment with no way of earning a living or in poor, overcrowded rural surroundings to which they adapted with great difficulty. Many eventually settled on the edges of towns such as Mbuji Mayi, whose population increased by 200,000.

Tension and uncertainty in Kivu

In Kivu, the eastern part of the country which shares borders with Rwanda and Burundi, tensions came to a head over the presence of Rwandese, some of whom had settled in the region before colonization, while others arrived during colonial rule or after independence. The last great wave of immigrants had consisted of Tutsis fleeing the "social revolution" of 1959. The first attacks on *non-originaires*, who make up around 80 percent of the population in the Rutshuru, Masisi and Goma areas, came in 1963-64, when the provincial authorities decided to exclude the so-called "Banyarwanda" from civil service posts in North Kivu. In 1972 a law granting Zairian nationality to all residents of the province eased tensions for a while. But tempers flared again in 1981 when the Zairian parliament debated a bill intended to repeal the 1972 act, which, fortunately, was not adopted. The nationality issue, which in Zaire essentially means the Rwandese question, re-emerged as a bone of contention in 1991, when the National Conference was convened. From the start of the talks, all the "Rwandese", grouped in one party, CEREA, were excluded from the conference. Looked upon as foreigners in their own regions, despite forming the majority, and frustrated by the lack of local representation — the ethnic minority groups (Hunde, Nande and Nyanga) occupied 48 percent of all local government posts —, the Banyarwanda (the Tutsis and the Hutus) formed a co-operative association, the MAGRIVI. From late 1991 this association began a campaign of civil disobedience, refusing to obey the local authorities or pay taxes, setting fire to local leaders' homes, spreading pamphlets inciting rebellion, etc.

However, the roots of the conflict were perhaps not so much ethnic or regional as economic and social. It was a clash between two ways of life — that of the livestock farmers, mostly Banyarwanda, and the "indigenous" arable farmers — in a particularly fertile region where pressure on the land was intense because of settlement by migrants from all over the region, even from as far afield as Uganda. Over the years, the dynamic and well-organized Hutu and Tutsi livestock farmers acquired more land, obtaining title to property around Goma and Kinshasa, by both legal and illegal means. All the elements of a major

ZAIRE, 1992-94: FORCED REPATRIATION OF KASAIANS
FROM KATANGA AND TENSIONS IN KIVU

confrontation were therefore in place, and some authorities no doubt played the ethnic card to regain control of the province, thanks to the clashes; Kivu, like Kasai, was traditionally opposition territory.

Trouble broke out on 20 March 1993, after one of the leaders of the MAGRIVI was arrested. By the end of April ethnic fighting had claimed between 2,000 and 3,000 lives and over 50,000 people, of all backgrounds, had fled their homes. Within a few months, estimates of the dead ranged from 6,000 to 15,000 and over 250,000 more were homeless. By early 1994, however, meetings were held to bring the warring factions together and there was hope that the cycle of violence might be broken and that the displaced might gradually be able to return to their villages. Despite the *rapprochement*, feelings still ran high and there was a constant risk that the situation would once more deteriorate into fighting. The fragile peace was threatened by the arrival of hundreds of thousands of Rwandese.

The sudden arrival of around a million refugees in the Goma area in early July 1994, and almost another 150,000 around Bukavu in late August when the French army left the "safe humanitarian zone" in south-west Rwanda, had dramatic consequences for the local inhabitants. In the space of a few days, both areas were flooded with refugees who filled all available open space, overwhelming the health services and water supplies and bringing cholera and dysentery with them. At the same time, food prices doubled and the streets became unsafe as Zairian soldiers seized new opportunities for plundering.

In addition to the lucrative racket of robbing refugees, who were relieved of their meagre belongings on crossing the border, the arrival of massive humanitarian aid was a godsend to an impoverished army that had become accustomed to living off civilians and had no qualms about using its weapons to intimidate aid organizations and take its cut of the aid intended for the refugees. Not to be outdone, the fleeing soldiers of the Rwandese armed forces redoubled their looting of refugee camps and sought to increase their control on the civilian population by discouraging would-be returnees from going back to Rwanda.

The longer the refugee problem lasts, the greater the risk of heightening tensions between the Banyarwanda and the local people and further destabilizing a sensitive region which could plunge into a new cycle of violence at any moment.

4

HAITI

On 29 September 1991, a coup unseated Haiti's first democratically elected president, who had come to power in December 1990. This brutal halt to the country's first experiment with democracy plunged the whole of Haitian society back into its traditional state of deadlock for three years. The future of this small Caribbean country, one of the world's poorest, now looks bleaker than ever. Having given its backing to the electoral process which had brought President Jean-Bertrand Aristide to power, the international community could not stand idly by, but its credibility was sapped by the lack of consensus among the countries most closely involved and the shortage of political will on the part of the West, notably the United States. After three years of half-measures and vacillation over economic sanctions and the handling of the boat people, the international community finally decided to use "all necessary means" to return the country to democratic rule. The US launched "Operation Restore Democracy" on 19 September by sending 20,000 of its troops into Haiti (a step approved by the United Nations Security Council on 31 July), and President Aristide returned on 15 October. The international community will need to move beyond the success of its first intervention and prepare for a long-term involvement.

◆

A society split in two

Haiti's independence on 1 January 1804 followed thirteen years of war between the French army and rebel slaves, and saw the country's new leaders (Haitian-born Creoles) having to cope with an economic blockade imposed by France and other colonial powers in fear of spreading unrest. Backed into a corner, they saw no alternative but to restore the old plantation system, but the former slaves, who were mostly African-born, refused to play along, turned on their new masters and fled to the mountains to fend for themselves.

A gulf rapidly opened between the two groups, and it remains to this day. On one side, the Creole minority turned the machinery of state into their personal fiefdom, and vied among themselves for power and control of the country's wealth; on the other, the Negroes became outcasts, were denied a voice and saw their regular uprisings bloodily put down. The new élite wanted to prove to the world that they were "civilized" and did their utmost to ape European court customs and project an image of belonging to a modern state. Meanwhile, out in the country, and later in the shanty towns, the majority of Haiti's inhabitants reverted to the old survival techniques and evasion of authority of colonial times, "heading for the hills" just as the fugitive maroon slaves had done before them. Haitian society's two halves were to go on living in their separate worlds, knowing nothing of each other and mired in mutual fear.

The last two centuries of Haiti's history are largely a product of this shaky start to independence. The Duvalier dictatorship (1957 to 1986) saw Haitian society at its most divided. François Duvalier ("Papa Doc") infiltrated every corner of the country's life, strengthening his position by dividing every family. The whole of Haiti was placed under tight control, with Duvalier recruiting his foot-soldiers, the notorious *Tontons Macoutes*, from all layers of society. Poverty and oppression kept most Haitians at subsistence level, as if history and the future were passing them by. Papa Doc's son Jean-Claude, who succeeded him in 1971, lacked his father's authority and ideological pretensions. This caused cracks to appear in the power structure; by the beginning of the 1980s the two halves of Haitian society were rubbing shoulders in Port-au-Prince, and radio stations and grassroots organizations were springing up everywhere. The physical opportunities for escape continued to be limited by population pressure, however. The young in particular (half of all Haitians are under 17 years of age) began to realize that the old tactic of "heading for the hills" would not work any more. Moving into politics, they played a decisive role in the uprisings that brought down Jean-Claude Duvalier on 7 February 1986.

This was the beginning of a long and painful transition, with a succession of coups and outbreaks of violence. Even with the dictator gone, the system passed down through two centuries remained intact. As had happened just after independence, the political class lapsed into endless in-fighting, which paved the way for the return of the army (long sidelined by Papa Doc).

The people enter politics

The have-nots gradually became involved in politics, and within a few years rejected the old order and demanded a say in Haiti's affairs. In 1990, Aristide translated these aspirations into action. While he lacked the stature and the policy platform of a statesman, he was at that point the only Haitian on whom the lower classes could focus their hopes for change. The significance of the wave of support for Aristide even in the first round of the presidential elections (he attracted 67 percent of the vote) was eclipsed by the revolutionary impact of a huge voter turnout, this from an electorate which had been denied a say in politics for so long and which was 85 percent illiterate. The presence of a United Nations observer mission (the first time the UN had assisted in elections outside the traditional framework of decolonization or dispute-settlement) obviously had a considerable psychological effect. On 7 February 1991, the day of the president's inauguration, Haitians spoke of a "second independence". The word "we" had come back into Haitians' vocabulary: the paintings which appeared on Port-au-Prince's walls proclaimed "Together we will rebuild our country".

The September 1991 coup

This momentum was halted by the bloody September 1991 coup led by General Raoul Cedras and provoked by the fear felt by an élite confronted with the arrival on the political scene of people it could see only as stereotypes. To ward off the danger, the ruling classes did not balk at buying the services of an army they had always mistrusted.

On the night of 29 September 1991 a massacre was carried out in the poorer sections of Port-au-Prince. Nobody was spared: men, women, babies and old people all fell victim to the blind brutality of soldiers travelling around in private cars which the rich and powerful later boasted had been lent by them. The killers even attacked those who had tried to organize help for the victims, and went as far as to finish off the wounded in the hospitals. The scale of the carnage went far beyond what could be explained away as a quelling of unrest. It was a message to the poor to abandon all hope. A flyer in Creole being circulated in Port-au-Prince in October 1991 said: "The poor must know that they are nothing [...] The poor must understand that doing away with flies, rats or poor people amounts to the same thing." Some of the élite echoed these thoughts in their own words, making it clear in interviews that it was unthinkable that the vote should be given to a load of ignorant and dangerous illiterates.

After three weeks of terror, blanket security was imposed in the true Duvalier tradition, although the *attachés* had replaced the *Tontons Macoutes*. For the next three years Haiti was not just in the grips of a fairly disciplined army, it was caught in a spider's web of security covering every neighbourhood of Port-au-Prince and every country district. The system hatched by Papa Doc, with its reliance on informers and blackmail, was still too recent not to be able to take up where it had left off. It was further shored up by groups of paramilitaries recruited from among the helpers of the old regime and traffickers of all descriptions. Summary executions, rape and killing sorties became commonplace in the poorer parts of town. The blacklist got longer by the day. The night of 29 September 1991 marked the beginning of a life outside the bounds of time and humanity for seven million Haitians.

Violence, poverty and political deadlock

Day-to-day violence also appeared in the guise of poverty. This was all the more insidious and shocking for existing cheek-by-jowl with the ostentatious wealth of a tiny minority, and all the more inhuman for sapping the very dignity of the poor. This poverty meant more than having no water or electricity and worrying about how to feed the children, it meant living in utter degradation ("the poor must know that they are nothing"). But the poor also had to be kept poor, and the military and their helpers ran rackets to make sure that this was so. The inhabitants of the poor neighbourhoods found it more and more difficult to survive, and society began splitting apart. Grassroots organizations and, more to the point, the Haitian family's traditional support systems were undermined. Being part of this situation, Haiti's politicians were just as unable to move on, bogged-down as they were in their thirst for power and money and their inability to envisage a society built in any other way. Even some of President Aristide's entourage (in exile first in Venezuela, then, after the coup, in the US) and political backers succumbed to this. The utter fragility of the country's political structure and the lack of reliable and credible representatives together sank the numerous attempts to reconcile the irreconcilable made since November 1991, chiefly through the UN. Even the Governors Island agreement of 3 July 1993, the only true attempt to break the deadlock, was signed without the two sides (Aristide and General Cedras) ever having met. The friction which arose at the end of 1993 within the presidential camp, between Aristide and his prime minister Robert Malval, speaks volumes about the difficulty of making compromises to get out of a situation whose solution demanded more than just the departure of the soldiers responsible for the coup.

Getting out

As the months progressed, the traumatized, despised and hopeless inhabitants of Haiti saw escape as their only chance of salvation. In the weeks immediately following the coup, over half a million people fled Port-au-Prince for the countryside. Yet others were later to travel in the other direction, moving from place to place in a long exodus within the country dictated by the ebb and flow of attacks on them. "Heading for the hills" had served its time as a solution, and those who could afford it took to the sea in flimsy, overloaded boats which were liable to sink in the first storm that came along. Approximately 60,000 boat people headed for the US. As a popular Haitian group sang in Creole "Open the door, I can't stand it any more". For a people without prospects, escape, however risky, seemed the only option in the face of an unremittingly bleak future.

The prospect of a massive exodus of Haitian boat people was undoubtedly what set the alarm bells ringing in surrounding countries, particularly the US, the desired destination of most of the escapees. Neither the government nor the public were willing to accept this eventuality. Haiti's crisis moved to centre stage in US domestic policy because of immigration (an issue which was becoming as sensitive there as it was in Europe) and because of the questions it raised about the credibility of US foreign policy (Washington had spent three years changing tack).

62

HAITI, JUNE 1994: DESIGNATED CENTRES FOR HAITIAN REFUGEES

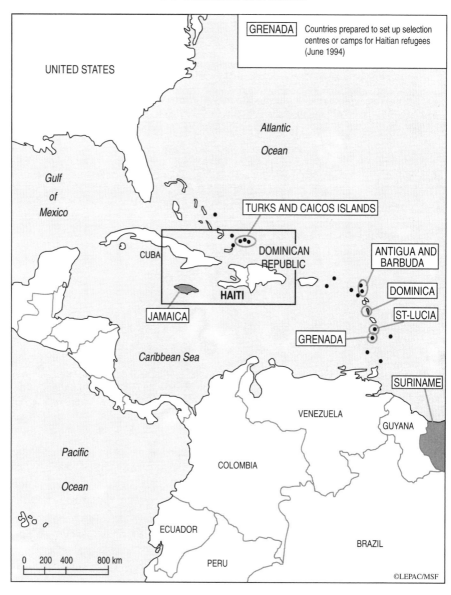

Sources: Collectif Haiti de France; National Coalition for Haitian Refugees; MSF.

Haiti, 1994: the boat peoples' route

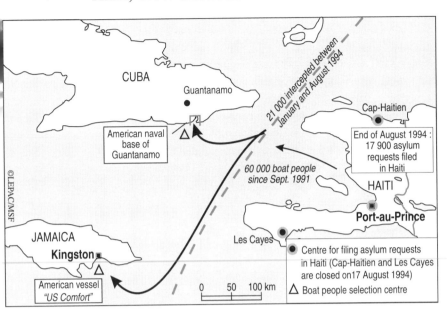

21 000 intercepted between January and August 1994

CUBA

Guantanamo

American naval base of Guantanamo

60 000 boat people since Sept. 1991

Cap-Haitien

End of August 1994 : 17 900 asylum requests filed in Haiti

HAITI

Port-au-Prince

JAMAICA

Kingston

American vessel "US Comfort"

Les Cayes

● Centre for filing asylum requests in Haiti (Cap-Haitien and Les Cayes are closed on17 August 1994)

△ Boat people selection centre

0 50 100 km

©LEPAC/MSF

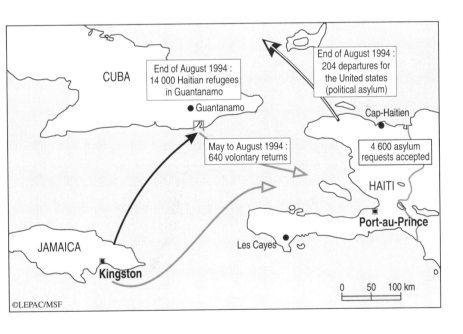

CUBA

End of August 1994 : 14 000 Haitian refugees in Guantanamo

● Guantanamo

End of August 1994 : 204 departures for the United states (political asylum)

Cap-Haitien

May to August 1994 : 640 volontary returns

4 600 asylum requests accepted

HAITI

Port-au-Prince

JAMAICA

Kingston

Les Cayes

0 50 100 km

©LEPAC/MSF

The first refugees to put to sea after the coup were intercepted by the US Coastguard and taken to the US base at Guantánamo Bay in Cuba, from where those who were granted refugee status were allowed to enter the US. Their numbers grew rapidly, however, and the Bush administration decided in May 1992 to repatriate them automatically without even giving them a chance to request asylum (something which breaches the principles of the 1951 Convention on the status of refugees). US human rights organizations tried in vain to defend the right of asylum and presidential candidate Bill Clinton made it a campaign issue, calling the policy illegal and immoral, and pledging to review it. Once elected he backtracked for fear of provoking an exodus to the US and announced on 15 January 1993 that the policy of turning the refugees back at sea would continue. It was only in the wake of pressure from his traditional allies (including black lobby groups) and much hesitation that President Clinton decided at the beginning of May 1994 to change his policy.

Haitian boat people became able to request asylum in the US, and were gathered together on boats where the administration attempted to sort the "genuine" refugees from the "fakes". This attempt to distinguish between would-be immigrants and refugees was a clear demonstration of the limits of the West's pragmatism: the one thing which all asylum seekers have in common, beyond their experience of economic difficulties and political oppression, is their lack of a future. Once this procedure was complete and the applicants' status has been determined, those classed as economic refugees were forcibly repatriated to Haiti, and those deemed to be genuine refugees (approximately 30 percent by June 1994) sent to Guantánamo Bay; they were not allowed onto the US mainland. Guantánamo Bay was no longer a transit centre but a "safe area" where the refugees were to be held until the situation in Haiti allowed them to return in safety. Their repatriation began once President Aristide returned to Haiti, under American protection

This new policy, which denied recognized refugees access to US territory, marked a change in the attitude to refugees. The recent course of US policy on the Cuban boat people is a case in point: Cubans used to be automatically admitted to the US by virtue of its traditional hostility to communist regimes in general and that of President Fidel Castro in particular. Since the agreement of 9 September 1994, this is no longer the case, and the Cuban refugees are treated just like the Haitians. The refugee issue was formerly considered to fall under the heading of human rights. It is now viewed in terms of pressure to migrate. The US wants above all to stem the flow, which explains the apparent contradiction between its readiness to condemn oppression and its reluctance to admit the boat people.

This shilly-shallying said a lot about Washington's embarrassment at this facet of the Haitian crisis, which itself lay at the root of the internationalization of the country's plight. It is the refugee problem rather than the wish to defend democracy which led the US administration to push for a comprehensive solution to the Haiti problem. The US has played a leading role since the beginning of the crisis while also seeking international backing and the support of the countries of Latin America.

Three years of vacillation

For more than two years, international initiative upon international initiative failed to get to grips with the situation. A few days after the coup, President Aristide addressed the Security Council, but no consensus was forthcoming and the UN went no further than to provide backing through the General Assembly for proposals from the member countries of the Organization of American States (OAS). The OAS members were themselves unable to agree on anything more than statements of principle and a clearly symbolic embargo. This absence of joint political will goes a long way towards explaining why action against the *junta* in Port-au-Prince was half-baked and late in coming. The trade embargo declared by the OAS on 8 October 1991 was not really enforced until the spring of 1993 (Resolution 841 of 16 June 1993), but it did produce rapid results, as the perpetrators of the coup signed the Governors Island agreement three weeks later. The sanctions were lifted, as planned, once the agreement came into force. This was in order to allow the transitional government to get to work, but it meant that there was no longer a way to pressure the military men into sticking to their side of the bargain.

The army was quick to take advantage, and at the end of October 1993 (when he was due to step down) General Cedras was still in power in Port-au-Prince. The UN Security Council reimposed sanctions, but this time the *junta* had taken preventive action and the situation, particularly where human rights were concerned, went downhill. The joint OAS-UN General Assembly civilian observer mission found it more and more difficult to operate, but the organizations' members seemed unconcerned. Indicative of the international community's lack of resolve was the incident involving

Three years of self-serving embargo

◆

The complete blockade of Haiti declared by the United Nations Security Council on 6 May 1994 came as a dreadful admission of failure: for three years the international community had been pretending to enforce an embargo. The cowardice of the major players in this situation undermined a sanctions policy which nevertheless turned out to have a devastating effect on the populace.

The immediate aftermath of the September 1991 coup gave a taste of things to come. During October, the Organization of American States (OAS) suspended trade and financial transactions, while the United States, France, Canada, Germany and Switzerland froze loans to Haiti. The EEC, however, a substantial trading partner, hid behind the clauses of the Lomé Convention which forbade trade discrimination against any signatory country, leaving a gap in what was already a somewhat feeble common front. The US, meanwhile, tried its best from February 1992 to engineer exemptions from the trade ban to suit its subcontractors in Haiti.

When the UN took over from the OAS in January 1993 and imposed across-the-board sanctions (sanctions had already been extended to fuel and arms in November 1992), the effects of the half-hearted measures of previous years only became more pronounced: paradoxically, the backers of the *junta*, the very people targeted by the embargo, made a lot of money by taking advantage of the shortages and gaining control of the country's trade through smuggling and black-marketeering. The general population sank deeper into poverty and lost hope in the face of what appeared to be stalling tactics on the part of the US. The death-blow to the international community's credibility came in the summer of 1993, when the embargo was strengthened by a naval blockade and a freeze on bank accounts, only to be lifted prematurely after the Governors Island agreement and then re-imposed after the *Harlan County* fiasco.

It was not until May 1994, after three years of improvisation, that genuinely effective steps were taken: a naval blockade was imposed, selective financial action targeted the *junta*'s entourage and relief supplies reached the most disadvantaged. Those three years had, however, destroyed even the informal economy and quashed the Haitians' hopes that their suffering might one day lead to the return of democracy.

the *Harlan County*. This US vessel had been due to land US and Canadian troops to conduct a programme of reform for the Haitian army (in line with the Governors Island agreement and as part of the UN Mission in Haiti, UNMIH), but was met by hostile demonstrations in Port-au-Prince. Without bothering to consult the UN or the OAS, Washington (unsettled by the death of eighteen US soldiers in Somalia the week before) ordered the ship to turn back. This climbdown in the face of a handful of demonstrators dealt a final blow to the credibility of the US Haitian policy, which had already been undermined by two years of vacillation and half-measures.

The spring of 1994 saw the international community seemingly ready to act again, as all opportunities for negotiation had been exhausted. After two years of a half-hearted embargo which had only made the poorest poorer and its intended victims richer thanks to the black market, the US, followed by Canada and France, finally decided to bring real pressure to bear on the *junta*. The decision was taken on 6 May 1994 to impose a full embargo enforced for the first time by a naval blockade and surveillance of the (hitherto very porous) border with the Dominican Republic. This was also the first time the US had taken direct action against the perpetrators of the coup or their financial backers (revoking visas and freezing private bank accounts) and isolated the country by suspending commercial flights and halting financial transactions.

"Support democracy"

Having gone as far as it could with its sanctions, the US was now faced with the prospect of military intervention, an eventuality which could no longer be side-stepped when it became clear that economic measures would not dislodge the *junta*. Having failed to take firm and coherent action in time, the US found itself in the uncomfortable situation of choosing between admitting defeat at the hands of a handful of coup-plotting soldiers and the risk of military action. It was a desire to restore credibility to a US foreign policy severely undermined by three years of hesitation and vacillation, rather than the wish to defend democracy in the Caribbean or even the wish to stem the flow of boat people, that convinced the Clinton administration of the need to intervene.

On 31 July 1994, following discussions with other members of the UN Security Council, and given their understanding of Russia's role in the "near abroad", the US received the international community's go-ahead to intervene in Haiti. Security Council

Resolution 940 broadened UNMIH's mandate and authorized the use of "all necessary means to facilitate the departure from Haiti of the military leadership [...] and the return of the legitimately elected president". This unprecedented resolution, authorizing as it did intervention in the internal affairs of a state outside the (traditional) setting of peacekeeping or the (more recent) setting of relief activities, paved the way for a US landing in Haiti despite the opposition of the countries of Latin America. The resolution provides for two phases: a "multinational force" (in practice almost entirely American) was authorized to intervene, then it was planned that the 6,000 UNMIH Blue Helmets would take over, but only after a "secure and stable environment" was established to bring about a return to civilian rule and a general election.

Following intense psychological preparation aimed at convincing the *junta* to withdraw in order to prevent casualties in an operation that had been unpopular with the US public from the very beginning, and after a last-ditch mission led by former US president Jimmy Carter had ensured at the eleventh hour that the military leaders would step down by 15 October, the US troops landed in Haiti on 19 September. Over a period of nearly a month, playing on the vagueness of the "Carter agreements" and exploiting their huge presence on the ground, the Americans gradually loosened the *junta*'s hold on the country and paved the way for a return to constitutional rule. On 13 October General Cedras left for Panama, and two days later President Aristide arrived back in Haiti.

Despite the apparent success of the first phase, this first international intervention to restore democratic rule raises many questions. The first relates to the transition between the US and UN forces. International involvement in Haiti typifies a new kind of operation in which the UN sanctions the intervention of a regional power (as happened with the US in Somalia, France in Rwanda and, though more ambiguously, with Russia in the Caucasus) pending the arrival of its Blue Helmets. In Haiti, as occurred in Somalia, maintaining order is crucial in this period of transition. The departure of the *junta* caused the army and police to disintegrate, although in some cases they remained operational in the countryside. The Haitian peoples' safety was further compromised by the lack of success of the weapons buy-back programme and the fact that the efforts to disarm the military men's helpers have been more symbolic than genuine in their effect.

The paramilitaries may still be a threat, but civilian rule will only be consolidated by attacking the severe economic and social problems faced by Haitian society. The international community has an important role to play in reviving the country's economy in the long term (beyond the lifting of sanctions approved on 16 October, the day after President Aristide's return, and a temporary interest on the part of donors). Three years of dictatorship and international isolation have left what was already one of the world's poorest countries in a state of collapse. Many businesses have closed, public services are run down, no infrastructure maintenance is taking place and trade has plummeted. Unless the end of the military regime rapidly results in better living conditions for the populace, the return of internationally sponsored democracy may not survive hope giving way to disillusionment.

Justice is another key to rebuilding Haitian society. The new government will have to go beyond the amnesty law voted through by the parliament, and reconcile the need to heal a deeply divided society with the need to bring back the concept of responsibility after three years of terror and impunity. The transition from dictatorship to democracy and lawlessness to law and order will undoubtedly be long and frequently threatened.

"Operation Support Democracy" may have succeeded in bringing back "the legitimate and constitutional authorities", but the international effort is in danger of being fraught with problems. Unless there is a genuine consolidation of the process going on now, the entire enterprise is likely to be short-lived. Outside intervention is generally an unsatisfactory way of solving political problems which by their very nature are determined largely by the internal workings of a society and the willingness of those involved on the ground to make a long-term commitment to dialogue and compromise. The international community can of course do much to help Haitian society overcome its difficulties, but this will only happen if it goes beyond military intervention and makes a lasting undertaking to back the slow process of national reconciliation and social recovery with a coherent and determined policy.

5

BOSNIA

The war that has raged in Bosnia for a little over two years since spring 1992 has claimed nearly 200,000 victims, most of them civilians, and forced more than three million refugees and displaced persons into exile. This conflict, Europe's first since 1945, began in April 1992, on the very day that the Republic of Bosnia-Herzegovina was recognized by the European Community and the United States. When Bosnian Serb forces, with the support of the Yugoslav federal army, quickly seized almost two-thirds of the new republic's territory, the Western powers initially appeared to acquiesce in this fait accompli, *confining their response to reopening Sarajevo airport and deploying Blue Helmets in an attempt to help those most in need. In 1994, however, confronted with a war of aggression whose protagonists continued to flout the fundamental values of the European democracies, seriously undermining the credibility of the United Nations, the international community finally decided to act. In February, a NATO ultimatum halted the bombardment of Sarajevo and loosened the Serb stranglehold on the Bosnian capital, and a UN-brokered agreement between Croats and Muslims put an end to the fighting in central Bosnia. The respite was to prove all too brief. The UN's pusillanimous response to the onslaught on Gorazde, in April, and NATO's paralysis in the face of the onslaught on Bihac, in November, have allowed the Serbs to obtain their main military objectives. Impotence has given way to resignation.*

◆

Sarajevo between war and peace

"We feel like game in a reserve, waiting for the start of the hunting season..."

This summer 1994, the third in twenty-seven months of war, the 280,000 inhabitants of the Bosnian capital were still surrounded, unable to bring themselves to believe that the lull in the shelling brought about by the NATO ultimatum of 9 February could really last. That day had marked a turning point in the West's attitude to the conflict; by then, the 22-month siege had already seen some 10,000 people — most of them civilians — killed by sniper fire, without eliciting any real response from Western governments, in spite of growing pressure from public opinion. It took the mortar bomb attack of 5 February on Markale market in the heart of the old town, which killed 68 people, to convince the West, chivvied by France and the US, to raise the stakes by issuing the first explicit threat to the Serb forces laying siege to the city. If, at midnight on 20 February, any of their tanks and guns remained within a 20 kilometre radius around Sarajevo, they would be subject to large-scale air attacks. The Bosnian forces were also required to surrender their heavy artillery in this exclusion zone to the Blue Helmets.

The carnage may have stopped but the siege continues. Since February, Sarajevo has been walking a tightrope between war and peace, and remains a divided city; some 20,000 people, forced to flee from Serb-controlled areas, are still in the uncomfortable position of being refugees in their own town. In April, after lengthy negotiations, a passage was opened up on the Bridge of Unity and Fraternity, allowing people with the stamina to complete the wearisome bureaucratic procedures to cross over to the other side to visit their families for the first time since the beginning of the war.

An agreement signed on 22 March with the Bosnian Serbs under the auspices of the United Nations Protection Force in Former Yugoslavia (UNPROFOR) paved the way for the reopening of a "blue route" to skirt Serb roadblocks by crossing the UN-controlled airport, thus enabling supplies to be trucked into the city. The return of commercial traffic had an immediate impact on black market prices: a litre of petrol, which cost 30 Deutsche Marks during the blockade, could soon be had for 10, while sugar, flour and oil prices fell by similar proportions. Supermarkets reopened, electricity and running water were restored for a few hours a day, and the city gradually began to live again; but paradoxically, the return to a semblance of normality only served to heighten people's feeling of imprisonment.

Most are unable to leave the city, even for short trips, as the Bosnian authorities, fearing an exodus of qualified people, refuse to issue travel permits. During the siege and the shelling, survival was a full-time occupation, involving interminable — and often life-threatening — queues just to get a little water. Every day people would have to scavenge for branches, roots or bits of wood to cook the relief agencies' rice or pasta on their balconies. To leave while the city was besieged, bludgeoned and bombarded would have been an act of betrayal, but now that the tension has subsided somewhat, the people of Sarajevo are finding it harder and harder to cope with a situation that seems hopeless. For many of them, it is only now, in this moment of relative calm, that they are beginning to realize just how much they have lost, and quite how bleak the future looks. This general disillusionment is compounded by fears of a fresh outbreak of fighting and another winter of hunger and deprivation.

When, towards the end of July, the Bosnian Serbs underlined their rejection of the peace plan proposed by the "contact group" of great powers (the US, Russia, the United Kingdom, Germany) by stepping up their acts of provocation, prices again soared on the Sarajevo markets. Suspensions of the humanitarian airlift and closures of the "blue route" by besieging forces keen to remind everyone that without their co-operation the city would receive no supplies, crystallized the unspoken fears of the people of Sarajevo, who once again started to store provisions in their cellars — just in case. Sporadic shelling has since substantiated their misgivings. If two years of war have taught Sarajevo and Bosnia anything, it is not to expect too much help from the outside world.

The Muslim-Croat peace

The other great event of 1994 was the US-brokered agreement of 18 March between the Bosnian Croats, with Zagreb again in the driving seat, and the Sarajevo authorities, for the creation of a Muslim-Croat federation in Bosnia, thus putting an end to a year of bloody fighting between these two former allies. Under pressure from the Roman Catholic Church and threatened with economic sanctions by the international community, the Croat president, Franjo Tudjman, performed an abrupt *volte-face* and withdrew his support from the most extreme Bosnian Croat faction, the "Herzegovinans", a group from the south-western part of

Bosnia-Herzegovina (where Croats are in the majority), who were seeking to emulate the Bosnian Serbs by creating a separate republic, which would eventually be attached to Croatia. Their strategy was not only to seize the town of Mostar, which before the war had been inhabited by Muslims and Croats in equal proportions, but also to terrorize the Muslim population into leaving the area.

In Mostar and on the left bank of the River Neretva, some 55,000 Muslims, packed into the cellars of ruined houses, were besieged and shelled virtually without respite for nine months by the HVO (Bosnian Croat Defence Council), with the backing of Zagreb. The death toll from this bombardment, more vicious even than Sarajevo's in that it was concentrated on a much smaller area and forced the population to live "like rats", without water and electricity and virtually without food, was 1,600. Outside Mostar, the Bosnian — mainly Muslim — army had many successes in the fratricidal war against the HVO, and did not balk at using terror tactics to force the Croat population to flee, especially in the areas of Travnik and Kakanj. By the time the cease-fire was announced on 25 February, the Croats retained control of only three enclaves in central Bosnia, Vitez, Zepce and Kiseljak, each besieged by the Bosnian army.

The first consequence of the creation of a Muslim-Croat federation in Bosnia, which was given concrete form two months later with the formation of a joint government, was to return traffic to the roads of central Bosnia. The restoration of regional trade, which until the outbreak of fighting between Croats and Muslims had met more than 70 percent of local markets' needs, improved the supply of food and other humanitarian requirements to an area in worse condition even than Sarajevo, which was at least receiving some form of supplies via the UN airlift. Some 800,000 displaced persons now living in central Bosnia, where they account for nearly one third of the total population, are entirely dependent on international aid. In October 1993, the UNHCR, the agency co-ordinating aid for former Yugoslavia, launched an emergency appeal "to prevent a major humanitarian disaster". Relief operations had to be carried out under impossible conditions, running the gauntlet of road blocks set up by all the different warring factions, who would regularly hijack part of the contents of aid convoys or subject them to all kinds of blackmail before allowing them to pass. As private stocks dwindled, even in the countryside where people had hitherto managed to survive in virtual self-sufficiency, it became essential to get humanitarian aid circulating freely again, and to open up other airports, starting with that of Tuzla in north-eastern Bosnia.

Tuzla: a lifeline to the outside world

Tuzla, an industrial town with a population of 700,000, a third of them refugees, lies at the heart of a pocket that is virtually cut off from the outside world. In the eyes of many Bosnians, Tuzla, more so than Sarajevo, has become the symbol of multi-ethnic Bosnian resistance, with not only Croats and Muslims but also many Serbs fighting side by side in its defence since the beginning of the war. Surrounded on three sides by Serb forces, the enclave was at one time receiving only 20 percent of its minimum requirements because of the fighting in central Bosnia. Sugar cost 35 Marks a kilo, flour 10 Marks, and it was almost impossible to find petrol. The Bosnian army held the airport, but the Serbs, whose artillery could shell the runway at will, refused to allow it to be used. With Russia acting as intermediary, the Security Council sought a compromise with the Serbs, and on 7 March a battalion of Scandinavian Blue Helmets took control of the airport. However, the reopening of the airport on 22 March 1994, when an UNPROFOR carrying Mr. Yasushi Akashi, the UN Secretary General's special representative for former Yugoslavia, and 22 tonnes of food, turned out to be more a symbolic gesture than anything else. Nevertheless, now that the fighting has stopped in central Bosnia, food convoys can once again get through. The Muslim-Croat pact has also put an end to the blockade of the Maglaj pocket, where for more than nine months humanitarian convoys were unable to reach more than 100,000 people besieged by both Serb and Croat forces.

Since the end of spring 1994, the situation has virtually returned to normal in the territory occupied by the Muslim-Croat federation, although civilian living conditions continue to be harsh and there are many doubts as to the future of this pact, which is still very fragile and subject to considerable tensions. Meanwhile, on the other side of the front line, in eastern Bosnia, the plight of the 120,000 people (many of them displaced by ethnic cleansing) living in the Muslim enclaves of Gorazde, Zepa and Srebrenica in Serb-controlled territory, has continued to deteriorate: designated "security zones" in May 1993 with the same status as Sarajevo, Tuzla and Bihac, and under the protection of UNPROFOR, these enclaves have become the main targets of the Serbs, who are anxious to eliminate the last pockets of Muslim settlement on their territory.

The tragedy of Gorazde

The Serb attack on Gorazde showed the limits of the resolve trumpeted by the international community two months previously in Sarajevo. Since the launch of the Serb offensive to the east of the capital in summer 1993, Gorazde has been cut off from Bosnian government-controlled territory and completely surrounded by Serb militia. On 29 March 1994, after a respite of several months, the Serbs started to bombard the enclave, which for two years has been home to about 55,000 people, half of them refugees from other towns in eastern Bosnia, such as Foca and Visegrad, where the ethnic cleansing was particularly brutal at the end of 1992. From the start of the offensive, UNPROFOR has played down the scale of the military operations in its daily reports on this security zone, a zone it is supposed to be protecting in accordance with Security Council Resolution 866. Nevertheless, it is patently obvious, as with Srebrenica in 1993, that the Serbs' objective is to clear all Muslims from an area they consider strategically important: Gorazde lies adjacent to the River Drina and borders on Serbia proper. On 5 April, the attacking forces breached the Bosnian lines and advanced to within four kilometres of the town. Life became a nightmare for the people trapped by the shelling, but despite the desperate pleas sent out by amateur radio, the besieged town's last remaining line of communication with the outside world, the international community remained almost totally indifferent, and the dozens of victims claimed daily by the Serbian onslaught went unnoticed. As far as the world is concerned, tragedies that are not televised do not take place.

In a town crammed with refugees fleeing the advancing Serbs, with the cellars already packed, there were few places left to hide. At the hospital, not far from the front line and hit by shelling daily, the wounded were piled up in the basement and medical staff had to crawl through the rubble to tend to them. With the West failing to respond, the Bosnian Serbs, commanded by Yugoslav army officers and supported by heavy equipment sent from Serbia and Montenegro, stepped up the bombardment. Then, on 11 April, NATO finally reacted by sending two US F-16s to bomb an old Serbian truck, a gesture which, coming so late in the day, felt more like an admission of weakness than a serious warning.

This air strike, the first carried out by NATO planes since the beginning of the conflict, was presented purely as a measure carried out in support of the dozen or so Blue Helmets who had entered the town a week earlier and were directly in the firing line; the

Gorazde, Sunday 17 April 1994
Eye-witness account by the MSF team

◆

"It is a disaster. After people's hopes were raised at the beginning of the week by the NATO air strikes on the Serb positions, morale has collapsed. Everyone now realizes that it wasn't enough to deter the aggressors, and that, on the contrary, it is Radovan Karadzic's threats that have deterred the United Nations. One year on, their promise to protect this security zone is shown to be worthless. Our only hope now is that there will be no massacre in the town.

"This morning you could already tell it was going to be quite some day. The first artillery shots were fired at dawn, as they have been every day for the last three weeks. But today, the explosions were louder, the volleys longer, the fighting nearer. There is talk of a meeting in Pale. Why? Who? There is talk of a cease-fire. By whom? With whom? There is no more time for idle chit-chat. UNPROFOR reports deliberately play down the gravity of the situation — it's as if the UN people are trying to avoid trouble, trying to slide out of their responsibilities. Meanwhile, the death list grows longer by the hour, to the accompaniment of tears and moans. This afternoon, the Serbs have come even closer to the hospital. Bullets are flying through patients' windows, mortars are exploding in the grounds. Casualty is full of injured people and corpses. The building is turning into a bunker, a target for the aggressors. What are we supposed to say to the people we work with, when they ask us if Europe has forgotten them?

"The tanks have entered the town, spreading panic among people already pushed beyond endurance. After the southern suburbs, it is now the turn of the north-eastern sections of the town to empty as people take refuge in the city centre. But the cellars are already full. Tonight, women and children will sleep in stairwells; it's all that's left to them. The world has abandoned them. The choice they face is simple: they can either die here, or start their lives again somewhere else. In spite of this, people are trying to keep their spirits up, trying to survive in the hope of being able to start living their lives again one day soon. How can you begin to explain the inactivity of the international community, after their repeated promises to protect the enclaves they renamed security zones? There is nothing more to be done here, nothing to be seen but the agony of people who just want to live."

protection of civilians did not appear to be on the agenda. Far from being deterred, the Serbs responded immediately by impeding UNPROFOR's movements around Sarajevo and tightening the noose round Gorazde. By 16 April, they were camped just outside the town, and controlled all the strategic points in the surrounding hills. A further air attack carried out soon after by British Sea Harriers was a complete disaster, with the shooting down of one aircraft. It was not until 22 April that NATO issued a genuine ultimatum, threatening the Serbs with air strikes if they did not withdraw to a distance of three kilometres from the city centre. Having achieved virtually all their objectives on the ground, the Serbs duly called a halt to their offensive and withdrew part of their heavy weaponry from the new 20 kilometre "exclusion zone" set up by NATO. According to the Bosnians, the offensive claimed 715 lives and injured nearly 2,000 people in just three weeks. Endorsing the Serb gains as a *fait accompli*, a battalion of Ukrainian and British Blue Helmets was finally deployed in what remained of the "security zone", now reduced to a tiny 200 square kilometres.

The people of Gorazde may have escaped a massacre by the skin of their teeth, but they now have no choice but to continue living in what has effectively become a large open-air camp, kept alive by whatever dribbles of humanitarian aid their Serb oppressors deign to let through. The precedent of Srebrenica, whose inhabitants live right on the edge, wholly dependent on humanitarian aid supplies that can be cut off at any time by Serb militia, does not leave much room for optimism. There are around 50,000 people in the town and the surrounding mountains, in an area reduced to 120 square kilometres. There is still no water or electricity, and apart from a few food aid convoys whose passage is subject to fierce negotiation, the Serbs allow no fuel or building materials through, thus undermining any hopes of rebuilding and returning to normal life. In the words of Murat Effendic, representative of the Srebrenica Crisis Committee in the Bosnian capital, "the Serb strategy is to keep reminding the people of Srebrenica that they have no future there, that their lives stretch to nothing more than basic, biological survival". The relief organizations still working in the enclaves are completely powerless to stop the tragedy that is literally unfolding before their eyes and have to engage in every sort of political/diplomatic haggling to get aid to the victims; they are the "social workers" of a vast open prison.

Ethnic cleansing pursues its course

Meanwhile, ethnic cleansing continues its grim progress. The Serbs' aim is to homogenize their conquests and, above all, make it impossible to reverse the situation by forcing the last Muslims and Croats remaining in Serb-controlled territory to leave before any peace plan could be implemented. The pressure and the exactions were stepped up after spring 1994, particularly in the area of Banja Luka, the Serb capital of north-western Bosnia and considered a Serb domain even before the war. In 1992, there were one million people living in the region, including 350,000 Muslims

BREAKDOWN OF NATIONALITIES IN BOSNIA-HERZEGOVINA
(based on the 1991 census)

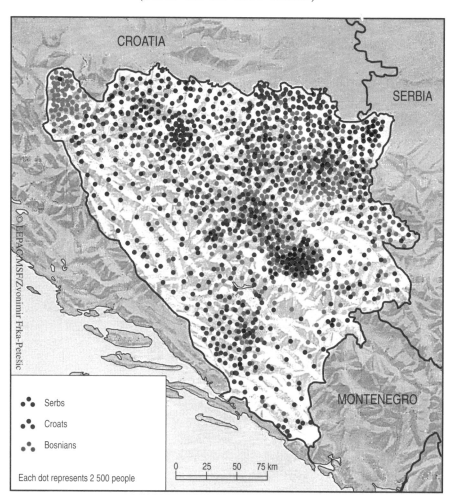

From an original map by Zvonimir Frka-Petešic.

and 180,000 Croats. According to the UNHCR, only 40,000 Muslims and 30,000 Croats remained in August 1994. All 200 of the area's mosques, several of them monuments from the Ottoman period, have been blown up, and new refugees are arriving in Croatia and territory held by the Bosnian army every day, fleeing from the violence and intimidation. In the neighbouring area of Prijedor, where 38 percent of the pre-war population was Muslim, the last remaining non-Serbs, by now no more than 5 percent of the population, were subjected to the same strong-arm tactics. In April, eighteen Muslims and two Croats were murdered in the space of a few days, making it clear to recalcitrant non-Serbs, and also

CONFLICT AND ETHNIC CLEANSING IN BOSNIA-HERZEGOVINA

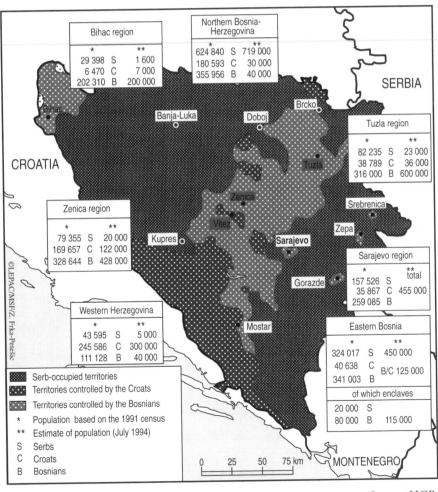

Source: HCR.

Map developed in collaboration with Zvonimir Frka-Petešić.

to humanitarian organizations reluctant to get involved in population movements, that the only viable solution was an organized departure. But when 6,000 people whose lives were under threat gathered in Prijedor to be bussed out by the International Committee of the Red Cross, the Bosnian Serb authorities changed their minds at the last minute and refused them permission to leave, apparently preferring to hold on to a few potential hostages.

And so it has continued, less visible but better organized than 1992's campaign of terror. Rather than simply being killed or thrown into camps, and having their homes destroyed outright, Muslims and Croats are instead subjected to an incessant barrage of discrimination, harassment and intimidation. At night houses are fired on or bombed, every now and then men will be killed and women raped, until even the most recalcitrant resign themselves to leaving. Private travel agents organize regular convoys into Croatia, but "candidates for departure" must first sign over all their possessions for a low price, pay their "debts" and find several hundred Marks to cover transport costs, exit visas and the taxes imposed by the Serb authorities. Profiteers and murderers have joined in an unholy alliance to make ethnic cleansing a lucrative business and, after more than two years of war, civilians continue to be threatened, terrorized, exploited, forcibly displaced, taken hostage and used for barter.

In the summer the ethnic cleansing programme continued in the Banja Luka region in north-western Bosnia, and was stepped up in the north-eastern part of the country, where in the space of three months 7,000 Muslims were expelled from Bijeljina towards the Bosnian government enclave of Tuzla. In Bosnia, forced population displacements are not simply the consequence of war, they are its main purpose, and the relief organizations are not only reduced to impotence by this strategy of terror, they are actually trapped into becoming its unwilling accomplices, as they sometimes endeavour to evacuate those whose lives are most at risk. In response to ethnic cleansing, which continues unabated in spite of the Security Council's regular condemnations, the humanitarian organizations again called on the international community to do something more than issue statements of intent and to make up its mind to take the requisite steps to put an end to it. But it is already too late. In the last two years, over 750,000 non-Serbs have been chased out of Serb-controlled Bosnian territory, notwithstanding the protests of the UNHCR and Red Cross. The militias are free to do what they like and the silence of the international community is overwhelming.

Diplomatic deadlock

Having so far failed to stamp out ethnic cleansing, the international community has tried to encourage attempts to find a political solution to the conflict. Heralded as the last chance to achieve this aim, the peace plan put forward on 6 July 1994 by the "contact group" of major powers, speaking for the first time with one voice, proposed giving the Serbs 49 percent of Bosnia (as opposed to the 70 percent they currently control), with the remaining 51 percent going to the Muslim-Croat Confederation. The deal was accepted immediately by the Sarajevo government, but rejected out of hand by the Bosnian Serbs, who appeared unimpressed by Western threats. The intransigence of the parliament of the self-proclaimed Republic of Bosnian Serbs and their president, Radovan Karadzic, caused a breakdown in relations with their allies and protectors in Belgrade. The Serb president, Slobodan Milosevic, openly endorsed the peace plan which, although not perfect, he felt consolidated most of the gains made on the ground. As proof of his goodwill, he immediately announced that he was severing economic and political ties with the Bosnian Serbs. Was this just another piece of play-acting, just as in 1993, when a similar embargo decreed after the Bosnian Serbs rejected the Vance-Owen plan was never actually enforced, or did it mark a genuine change of policy? It must be remembered that, in addition to the pressure being brought to bear by Russia, the Serbs have become weary after two years of economic sanctions. Milosevic appeared to be aware of the realities of the stand-off, and of the Serbs' inability to sustain a long war, particularly if the arms embargo on the Bosnians were to be lifted. At certain key strategic points, such as the Brcko corridor to the north, which links the Serb territories in Bosnia and Croatia to the mother country, Greater Serbia is no more than half a dozen kilometres wide.

The Bosnian authorities, led by President Alija Izetbegovic, only accepted the peace plan proposed by the "contact group" because they knew their adversaries would not. They feared that a peace plan, even one accepted by both parties, would simply preserve the status quo, to the benefit of the Serb militias, and that it would be a long time before any changes would be implemented on the ground. The precedent set by Croatia would seem to justify this pessimistic view: two years after the deployment of 14,000 Blue Helmets in the Serb-held quarter of the country under the Vance plan, the 419,000 refugees expelled from the area have yet to return to their homes and the Serb militias have still not been disarmed.

The failure of this latest attempt to find a political solution led to a resumption of hostilities in November 1994. As happened in the cases of Srebenica in February 1993 and Gorazde in April 1994, the Bosnians' desperate attempts to widen the Bihac enclave have served as a pretext for a renewed offensive on the enclave. In the absence of any international reaction, apart from a few symbolic NATO raids, Serbian forces have taken control of part of the "security zone" in violation of UN Security Council resolutions. This not only underlines the impotence of the UN but also weakens the credibility of NATO's dissuasive capacity. The split between Europe and the US has paralyzed the Western powers and dulled their last remaining pangs of conscience about Bosnia: everything points to acceptance of the *fait accompli*.

II
Opinion

6

GENOCIDE IN RWANDA: WE CAN'T SAY WE DIDN'T KNOW

by Rony Brauman

Ever since the concentration camps were discovered at the end of the Second World War, the West has held fast to a belief that reality has failed to shake. We must remember that it was only because the Final Solution was planned and implemented on the quiet that it was possible in the first place. We did nothing because we knew nothing. Realization would have come quickly if it had been possible to find out what was going on. In short, it was not knowing, rather than not caring, that resulted in nothing being done.

We won't dwell on what the historians tell us about the Allies' information at the time, as the significance here lies not so much in the actual facts as in the message people draw from them, namely that to know is to be in a position to act, and knowing is therefore tantamount to doing something. This self-deception should by rights have been shattered by the glaring evidence provided by a succession of events from 1945 to 1989. It was not. Seeing the invasion of Budapest and the building of the Berlin Wall, and the tales of the Gulags in the former Soviet Union or the Khmer Rouge actions in Cambodia certainly dented the influence of Communism, but did nothing to alter the political attitude of democratic nations. Nor did they arouse a ground swell of opinion. The belief that nothing could shake the post-war world order (shored up by clouded reasoning, a need for illusion and the connivance of the intellectuals) goes a long way to explaining the sloth of the times.

With the end of the Communist era, the future looked ready to take on a different shape. Yesterday's reluctance — whether right or wrong — seemed to be paving the way to tomorrow's new resolve. The Gulf War and "Operation Provide Comfort" heralded a new world order whose buzzwords were *human rights, solidarity* and *democracy*. Despots had no choice but to hold tight. On the eve of the third millennium the unfulfilled promise of the 20th century was at last in the process of being made good: advances in knowledge and conscience were going to keep pace with each other.

Notwithstanding this, it took two years for the ethnic cleansing campaign waged by Bosnia's Serb nationalists to be exposed for what it was: a fascist conquest. Rather than face up to their responsibilities, the governments of Europe spent those two years playing the humanitarian card for all it was worth in order to prove that a new era had arrived. Doing our humanitarian duty for the victims took our minds off our political duty to deal with the torturers. The smoke screen has now outlived its usefulness, however, and the ability of the relief effort to deflect attention from our political responsibilities is waning. The ultimatums given to the Serb militias in Sarajevo and Gorazde in February and April 1994 are a salutary sign that the changes for which the relief workers are pushing is on the way, making it less likely that accusations of using the ambulance approach will stick. The fact remains that once the smoke screen of good intentions is blown away, it becomes clear that ethnic cleansing is continuing to the indifference of many.

As the political scientist Pierre Hassner points out, "The fact that the barbarism reported by the media sometimes strikes the international community as unacceptable and moves it to protest and act when starvation and genocide occur in the increasingly common instances in which not caring cannot hide behind not knowing, is evidence of the appearance of a glimmer of a conscience driven by a world vision, pacifism, the environment and humanity. That this should produce an objective and moral consensus and legitimacy capable of winning over the warring parties, settling their differences and judging and punishing their violence and crimes. And that the international community should be represented by the UN which in turn should be represented by the Security Council can be considered nothing short of an illusion, however."[1] Freed from the moral and political dogmas which portrayed compassion as a guilty weakness, the societies of the industrialized nations have in the last twenty years evolved new forms of

---

1. Pierre Hassner, "Les impuissances de la communauté internationale", *in Vukovar, Sarajevo...*, Éd. Esprit, Paris, 1993, p. 88.

solidarity which are undeniably positive. It should be remembered, however, that this world conscience is something that has been around since the beginnings of the humanitarian movement. Gustave Moynier, the chairman of the Red Cross, wrote as far back as 1885 that "these days we know what is going on in every corner of the globe. News of the slightest skirmish spreads like wildfire, all but putting the dying on the battlefield in front of the reader".[2] In its transition from telegraph to satellite and after-the-event to live reporting, news has speeded up to the point where it is virtually instantaneous. Today's fantasy of making news in the global village the preserve of everyone and thus producing a world conscience seems to have produced a belief that moral conscience has always been part of us, as if it went hand-in-hand with being conscious.

In any event, the media told us what was happening in Rwanda even as the pogroms began in April 1994. Everyone should in theory have been capable of making the connection between these events and the similar massacres orchestrated by the Rwandese regime in earlier years which were exposed by the press and human rights organizations. The eruption of violence was shown to a world-wide audience with the information at its disposal to see that what was happening was a campaign of extermination. In this instance we could not say we didn't know. For two and a half months, Hutu extremists were, nevertheless, able to commit genocide (televised live) without the international community doing anything more than arranging for Europeans to be evacuated and producing a few Security Council resolutions calling for an end to the violence. The killers of Rwanda turned their country into a slaughterhouse completely unimpeded, and caused carnage as extensive as that wrought by the *Khmers Rouges* in four years. Bosnia provided a foretaste of what Rwanda was to prove to us: this tragedy has undermined the last of the optimistic post-war illusions. We could have been watching Auschwitz live.

It could be countered that France *did* react. Although too little, too late, "Operation Turquoise" saved face. However, it failed to stop the genocide. This technically successful and initially unjustly criticized undertaking saw thousands of refugees protected by French soldiers. Moved by more than just the desire to draw a veil over its responsibility for propping up a regime with fascist leanings, France undoubtedly scored by propelling the international community beyond its role as the chronicler of horror. Nevertheless, contrary to what is claimed all too readily, it was the

---

2. Alain Destexhe, "De Solférino à Sarajevo", *Projet*, spring 1994.

military defeat inflicted by the Rwandese Patriotic Front (RPF) on the old regime, and not the French intervention, which brought a halt to the massacres.

It was a duty of human decency that dictated that the perpetrators of the genocide should be stopped and their death machine disabled. It was a duty to provide relief that dictated that those who had escaped the massacres and (more generally) all the victims of this terrible chaos should be helped. Although these duties were not incompatible, what happened was that the provision of relief made it possible to forget the concern for human decency by masquerading as just such decency. This explains the bitter disappointment of all those (especially the Non-Governmental Organizations, NGOs) who had pressed that need home. Despite statements from the UN Secretary General, Mr. Boutros Boutros-Ghali, the French Head of State, François Mitterrand and the French minister for Foreign Affairs, Alain Juppé, and despite a very clear report from the UN Commission on Human Rights, the Security Council failed to recognize that genocide was taking place. The reason for this is simple. Recognition of the fact that the genocide was occurring would have meant taking military action to end it, less as a result of the Convention on the Prevention and Punishment of the Crime of Genocide (who pays any attention to humanitarian agreements?) than as a result of public reaction. Unable to bring themselves to answer the question, the world's movers and shakers decided in their wisdom not to ask it. One could wonder what precedent there was for invoking a duty of human decency. What had the international community ever done to suggest that such a duty (as opposed to the individual interests hiding behind it) actually existed? The only things which hinted that this kind of duty might be there were pious official statements and virtuous lectern rhetoric, supported by the idea that technical progress somehow brings moral progress. As officialese is by definition unaffected by the reality it purports to describe, we can bet that the gulf between action and words that we have seen will be quickly bridged, if this has not happened already.

The exodus of hundreds of thousands of Rwandese to Zaire and the ensuing cholera epidemic provided the international community with an opportunity to forget the cynicism with which it had abdicated its own self-imposed duties. The outpouring of humanitarian concern reached its zenith in July 1994, with cameras, ministers, civilians and troops from the world over arriving to do heroic battle with the outbreak of disease. The people who had sat stony-faced while innocents were massacred were suddenly deeply moved by the damage wrought by a bacterium.

The miraculous and unheralded arrival of dysentery gave the world a born-again virgin purity. Genocide took a back seat to a humanitarian disaster. The drama of the rescue could now begin, and the curtain of good intentions allowed to fall on the mass graves. The moral and political question mark created by the world's passive acquiescence to the annihilation of the Tutsis was erased by the monumental logistical problems of dealing with the epidemic. Genocide, the ultimate evil, the crime of crimes, had found the perfect camouflage not in concealment and silence, but in noise and fanfare; not in negation of the evil, but in displaying the misfortunes it caused. In its new clothes, the extermination campaign waged by a regime friendly to the French was consigned to the category of unfortunate events, joining many others as one more tragedy to add to those of the past. It became yet another international report of the kind which invariably seems to be used to describe day-to-day events in Africa. This was (in the unashamed journalese of Security Council Resolution 929) a "humanitarian crisis". Why not rename the Kristallnacht a "window crisis" and the policy of rape which occurred in Bosnia a "gynaecological crisis"?

Empty of meaning though it is, this wording has a practical message: all suffering is created equal. Our times are no worse than any that have gone before, but they *do* make double-speak a centrepiece of the way they see the world. Humanitarian to the core, the international community has pushed the morality of the emergency as far as it can go by declaring itself neutral in the face of genocide. This it has accomplished firstly by portraying it as an ethnic war in which everyone has been fighting everyone else and in which no sensible person could take sides, and secondly by portraying it as a humanitarian disaster in which anybody and everybody is an actual or potential victim. That cholera strikes murderer and victim alike (sacrificing them as if to quench our thirst for compassion) is beyond dispute, however.

Does this mean that the refugees of Goma should be left to die as a protest against the world's indifference? Of course not. The armed forces, the international organizations and the NGOs have worked together to implement this vital rescue operation, as well they should have done. Help has come to not a few murderers, but it has also come to many more innocent people, and this is what counts. We cannot allow the genocide be played down or fogotten in the burst of the international community's self-congratulation for a "job well done" in the refugee camps.

Once again, the duty of human decency (or rather the sentimentality which saps our capacity for outrage and masquerades as human decency) has enabled the world to disregard morality. "We knew nothing so we did nothing" is an excuse which could have been used when the Nazi death camps or the Khmer Rouge killing fields were discovered. One of the century's biggest massacres was broadcast live across the world and this means that the didn't know argument doesn't work any more. Political leaders will have to find another justification for their failure to act. The best of these justifications — one which at any rate seems to have some mileage left before it is exhausted and replaced by another — is that of humanitarian duty. Humanitarian activity (valued by the powers-that-be as an instrument of brainwashing) is now the weapon of choice for governments and the UN in their efforts to turn the pitiful remains of politics into an equally pitiful media banquet. "Humanitarian" can be attached as an adjective to almost anything in order to fudge issues, cloud reason and cynically manipulate the need for relief. It cannot be denied that for anyone who sees politics as a form of public relations, humanitarian activity has become an effective way of communicating.

Progress must be given its due where it exists, however. In the 19th century, England would seize ships carrying cargoes of ebony (i.e. slaves) using the humanitarian principle that slavery was illegal as a pretext. This provided the country with a moral excuse to demonstrate that Britannia did indeed rule the waves. At much the same time, the massacres between Christians and the Druze, a religious sect, under the indulgent eye of the Ottomans in Lebanon gave rise to public protest, press campaigns and petitions in France. Despite the efforts of Great Britain, which backed the Druze, Napoleon III was given a mandate by the European powers, to send out an expeditionary force to gather the refugees and help them to rebuild their villages. Even if it failed to save its traditional protégés, France did reinforce its strategic position in a disputed area. Again during this period, Henri Dunant established the International Committee of the Red Cross in a bid to depoliticize humanitarian activities. He can hardly be blamed for having failed to foresee the reversal which some persist in seeing as progress. At the time, humanitarian activities were used to dress up bids for power. Today they are used to dress up powerlessness.

7

RWANDA : WHY MÉDECINS SANS FRONTIÈRES MADE A CALL FOR ARMS

by Guy Hermet

The humanitarian rationale requires the indiscriminate relief of all suffering. Its underlying principle is neutrality, a principle which denies knowledge to aid workers of the presence of fugitive murderers, unrepentant of their crimes, amongst those they protect or whose lives they save. There are however extreme circumstances in which this code of silence becomes untenable and international aid workers are forced to challenge the principle of neutrality. It is abundantly clear that the Rwandese tragedy can be classed among those landmark events in which the perpetrators of massacres cease to be "normal" killers and become the terrible engineers of a new holocaust differing from its predecessors only by virtue of its lightning speed. It is commonly agreed now that what began in Rwanda on 7 April 1994 was this century's fourth instance of genocide after the slaughter of Armenians during the Great War, the extermination of the Jews in World War II and the genocide of their own kind by the Khmer Rouge in Cambodia. Taking this one step further, if there is some question of the "genocidal" nature of the suffering of the Armenian people, for all its horror, or of the crime committed in Cambodia, there can be no doubt that what the Tutsis and Jews have experienced are two versions of the same truly ethnic holocaust. It was the extreme nature of this tragedy that obliged Médecins Sans Frontières to take a stand, cast aside its humanitarian neutrality and clamour for military intervention in full knowledge of the risks entailed in "armed humanitarianism".

Humanitarian rationale and political logic

It is clear that, even when driven by disinterested motives, states cannot forsake their political preoccupations. It is in the nature of any state worthy of the name to give absolute priority to the preservation of its power and to its prosperity, security and prestige, both inside and outside the country it embodies. While governments also lay claim to certain moral principles and see to their enforcement, these principles only really come into play insofar as they tally with national interest, especially if they require the use of armed force. The fact that there is no such thing as a perfectly rational state further complicates the matter. The state is not a logical abstract concept. It is what the men who govern it make it. On the one hand its action is subordinate to their personal moral reflexes, to the commitments they wish of it even if no tangible benefits are accrued by the state. On the other hand, and there's the rub, politicians inevitably transform their state into the instrument of their short-term calculations. They turn its action to their advantage and their decision is partly guided by "vote-catching" considerations. These constraints, which are tied in with political responsibility, in its optimum sense, and motivations, which are far more questionable, converge to a point where pure mixes with impure, generosity with hypocrisy and humanitarianism with short-termism, as in our present case.

Operation "Restore Hope" in December 1992 is one such example. While the American fleet was landing in Somalia, the US government saw fit to ignore the equally terrible tragedies in Liberia, southern Sudan and Afghanistan. What explanation is there for this deliberate choice other than its timing and political rather than humanitarian context? The American military intervention in Somalia took place in time to give President Bush, nearing the end of his term in office, the opportunity for an end-of-administration swan-song — a patriotic, philanthropic gesture which could not fail to appeal to the national pride of his fellow Americans. Experts calculated that the cost of this operation in terms of men and resources would be low as the Somalis were only a rag-tag bunch that would take off at the first alarm. This was the thinking behind the decision, but the reality proved somewhat different. In the meantime, nobody seemed concerned about the long term results or what will happen when the Marines leave Somalia. Obviously the overriding consideration was the immediate political gain to the United States, not the humanitarian outcome. But who was prepared to stand up and be counted when it mattered? Although the use of force is unable to offer a lasting solution, it can save tens of thousands of lives over a period of weeks or months. That is what seems to count above and beyond criticism, which is considered indecent.

The events in Rwanda are symptomatic of the same reasoning in the case of military action by France. If the French government's indignation at the genocide was sincere, why then the "no-comments" and acts sometimes unworthy of a state? Why the complicity with the Hutu killers even in early April 1994, and the delayed military operation designed to restore France's tarnished reputation but which, in fact, found only mass graves already covered and actually protected the fleeing hordes of murderers by offering them the safe haven of the sanctuary guarded by its own troops?

Confusion about the application of the epithet "humanitarian" to military action is not just a recent phenomenon. Between 1815 and 1950 humanitarian motives were constantly called on to justify colonial conquests and other forms of armed intervention in Africa, Asia, Latin America and on the high seas. In the 19th century, Great Britain granted itself the right, with the clearest of consciences and cheered on by all the altruist spirits of the age, to inspect ships from all over the world in the hope of catching slave traders red-handed. Such action ensured that liberal Britain's contribution to the fight against slavery was decisive. But it was equally concerned with consolidating its position as the, then, most powerful nation in the world. Thus gunships were dispatched by Britain and the other nation powers to help the missionaries with their task of teaching the "savages" good manners, a task for which they were shown little gratitude to reward their self-sacrifice. The gunships gave way to regiments which put a stop to the tribal wars and helped the colonial administrators complete their civilizing mission.

So where are we now? Colonization is no longer in vogue but the old idea is gradually coming into favour again of a sort of long-term guardianship over the turbulent regions of sub-Saharan Africa or even a country like Haiti, regions where the minimum conditions of personal, health and food security ceased to apply along with the state's authority. Is it really so hard to remember that this solution has already been tried on the countries "mandated" to the League of Nations and later to the United Nations, and that it was nothing if not colonialism by other means? Has it not occurred to anybody that future mandates might be carried out by the representatives of the wealthy countries, financed with their money, and that this is bound to provoke the same degree of resentment as the former colonial domination? In view of the above, don't you find that the recent military-cum-humanitarian interventions have the ring of that frightful brand of saintliness for which humanitarianism is only the label it tags on its own good deeds?

Aid workers in a quandary

These facts are disturbing but, where Rwanda was concerned, Médecins Sans Frontières could not afford to leave it at that. Genocide was taking place in front of a world-wide audience while governments sat idly by. Weeks of inaction went by although every minute counted and the Hutu murderers carried out their systematic plan to exterminate the Tutsis. It was time for a humanitarian *volte-face*. Not to insist on the use of any means to stop the killers in their tracks would have been a criminal act in itself and would have left Médecins Sans Frontières open to the same accusation levelled at the International Red Cross during World War II when it refrained from revealing the abomination of the Nazi extermination camps for fear of losing its scope for operations in Germany, especially in the prisoner-of-war camps.

The first step was the hardest. France was the sole country capable of military intervention in Rwanda at short notice, but its government had compromised itself more than most with the regime that orchestrated the atrocities. It is pointless to go into the whys and wherefores: for trivial but nevertheless disgraceful motives, France had remained President Juvénal Habyarimana's faithful ally to the last. All the more sinister then that the exterminations were known to have been perpetrated by militias armed by the Rwandese armed forces which had been trained only weeks before by French military advisers. There's no surprise therefore that the Rwandese Patriotic Front (RPF), with a Tutsi majority, should consider French soldiers its sworn enemies for providing the guns that were firing on them. Moreover, going back to the chain of events again, Médecins Sans Frontières had apparently taken a stance, admittedly in different circumstances, against the US intervention in Somalia and, prior to that, on the use of UN peacekeepers to protect humanitarian convoys in Bosnia. And now, just eighteen months further on, it was all change. Here was Médecins Sans Frontières launching a campaign for the use of force in Rwanda while the other organizations were advocating the moral and political impossibility of intervention by a French army which had only just finished training and arming the very people behind the assassination squads. The contrast was somewhat startling but this course of action was always founded in intrinsically sound logical arguments. In the final analysis, the fact is that the dilemma was insoluble in political terms but could only ever have one outcome in humanitarian terms. The atrocities had to stop before all else and, in view of the desperate urgency, there could be no qualms about the methods used.

Adopting this stance does not detract for one moment from the agonizing that the Rwandese tragedy caused and is still causing Médecins Sans Frontières and other humanitarian organizations. As far as both military and unarmed humanitarian action is concerned, the challenge now posed by the problem of equal treatment for both sides must not at any rate contribute to helping either indirectly or unintentionally the routed Hutu extremists (reminiscent of the way the UN peacekeepers acquiesced in the Serbian conquests in Bosnia and Croatia). The murderers cannot of course be aided on the same terms as the victims, knowing that neutral aid fairly dispensed to the two camps means giving an unexpected lifeline to the Hutu militiamen, who are keen to keep the refugees under their control until they are in a position to seize power again and maybe even finish off the massacre of their Tutsi enemies. Humanitarian aid might provide this lifeline if due care is not taken. The killers have already seized humanitarian supplies to help build up their control over the people or to resell them to keep the war machine going. Such unintentional support can also prove to have a political dimension, as deliveries of relief consignments have to be negotiated and the fact of negotiating is in danger of being presented as international recognition or even rehabilitation. This was borne out at the huge refugee camp at Benako on the Tanzanian border. The former ruling power took control of the camp and turned it into a rearguard base or sanctuary with reconquest in mind. The same phenomenon also occurred in the "Operation Turquoise" area and in the refugee camps of Goma, Zaire.

In May and June 1994, the international community allowed itself to be paralyzed by fear of the undesirable and unavoidable side-effects of intervention. To be blunt — this was not the time to stall. The first priority was to launch an urgent military intervention to stop the killing and then — and only then — start to worry about the constant risk which inevitably accompanies humanitarian action, i.e. the need to enter into contact with criminals, in this case the most heinous of all. Now is the time to insist that the perpetrators of genocide are never in a position to murder again, that they be sought out and brought to trial out of respect for the memory of their victims, thus ensuring that the word "humanitarian" retains its meaning as something more than mere gestures of basic compassion. But this is not the end of the story, other atrocities may be committed in the near future, other people continue to live under the threat of death. Where genocide is concerned, it requires more than military operations to cleanse the wound and more than dressing to heal it.

8

HUMANITARIAN LAW: ALL BARK BUT NO BITE

by Françoise Bouchet-Saulnier

In the history of the United Nations, 1994 will be remembered as the year that international humanitarian law was reinvented. In their interventions in Iraqi Kurdistan and in Somalia, the UN organizations invoked a revolutionary "right to interfere on humanitarian grounds". But the use of international force was still based, in law, on the existence of "threats to international peace and security" rather than on the suffering of civilians. With the conflicts in Yugoslavia and Rwanda, the UN has rediscovered the existence of international humanitarian law and is demanding its application. For the first time since World War II, the UN Security Council has set up an international war crimes tribunal to try the perpetrators of serious violations of humanitarian law committed in former Yugoslavia. There have been calls for the same solution to be implemented in Rwanda.

When the international community's most political body is so suddenly converted to the virtues of humanitarian law, we can only rejoice with caution. The legal instruments for ensuring that the atrocities of World War II never recur — adopted between 1945 and 1949 under the aegis of the UN — have lain unused for forty years. Although the proclamation and adoption of humanitarian law eased consciences in 1949, today's atrocities prove that these were empty words.

In order to understand and appreciate the current initiatives in the field of international justice, we must not forget the long and bloody chronicle of legal tricks and manœuvring that have gone on in the "world freed from the scourge of war" which the UN has been creating for us since 1945.

The law disarmed

Today, humanitarian law is used by the UN as a verbal bulwark against the barbarism and chaos spreading in some parts of the world. The invocation of international law has become the weapon of choice. After fifty years of oblivion, the concept of humanitarian law is now part of our political vocabulary. There is a tendency to cling to humanitarian principles in order to give wars a more human face, to dissuade criminals and to provide a framework for community life in an international community in a state of flux.

However, invoking humanitarian law is becoming increasingly derisory, as the only force behind this law is the force of words. The UN has adopted resolutions without providing the means for implementing them or any sanctions for their non-implementation. In former Yugoslavia, three and a half years after the beginning of the conflict, the UN machine has shown that it is capable of producing a legal discourse, without ensuring either action or justice.

In 1992, the UN's Special Rapporteur for former Yugoslavia, Tadeuz Mazowiecki, was given a mandate to monitor violations of human rights. He ascertained that there were massive, repeated and generalised human rights violations by all parties involved in the war. However, his report was notable in that it showed how the crimes committed in this war were of a different order. No sooner had he shown the existence of crimes against humanity than the UN machine went into action. A series of resolutions led to the creation of a committee of experts to carry out the same enquiry. Then, in light of the undeniable nature of the verdict rendered, an *ad hoc* criminal court was set up. However, two and a half years after the truth was established and a year and a half after the creation of the international tribunal, impunity and inertia undermine the principles each day. Despite all the expressions of shock and outrage, ethnic cleansing has taken place, has been witnessed on an ongoing basis, continues to occur and still goes unpunished. In short, the inadmissible is being allowed.

Thus, a new type of balance of power is emerging in international diplomacy between those who are full of promises and those who are still waiting for the money and political will to put these promises into action.

United Nations action in Rwanda illustrates perfectly the hypocrisy of UN resolutions. The UN Mission of Assistance to Rwanda (UNAMIR), which was set up on 5 October 1993, was given a mandate to contribute to the security of Kigali. At that time, it had a staff of 2,500 men. When the massacres began on 6 April 1994, the UN and the Western countries considered evacuating their personnel who were under the threat of violence. Within hours, the necessary reinforcements needed to evacuate the 3,000 westerners present in Rwanda were found. On 21 April, with the massacres in full swing, the Security Council washed its hands of the matter. Then, with its Resolution 912, it redefined UNAMIR's role and means. The Mission's staff was reduced from 2,000 to 270 soldiers, and its new task was to serve as an intermediary between the parties and to oversee and report on the evolution of the situation. Surely this was enough to throw down one's blue helmet in despair.

On 16 May, in light of the ongoing massacres and the enormity of the carnage, the Security Council gave UNAMIR a new mandate. Its mission was now to guarantee the security and protection of endangered civilians in Rwanda. On the basis of Chapter 7 of the UN Charter, the Security Council authorised UNAMIR to use force to protect threatened persons and sites as best it could. The question of whether force could be used — which had long been detrimental to the work of the peacekeeping forces in former Yugoslavia and in Somalia — appeared to be decided.

However, appearances can be deceiving. Although the Security Council had agreed to increase staff from 250 to 5,500 men, it would be four months, thousands of massacres and countless UN resolutions later before the additional troops arrived. Until then, UNAMIR would be unable to put its brand new mandate to the test.

Having failed to stop the genocide, the UN proceeded with a legal offensive against its perpetrators. On 28 June 1994, René Degni-Ségui, the Special Rapporteur of the UN Commission on Human Rights submitted his report of enquiry and his verdict. The victims died as a result of genocide and, to a lesser extent, because of the lack of UN assistance. The legal shadowplay enacted during the Yugoslav conflict had resumed.

On 1 July 1994, the Security Council requested the creation of a special expert group to verify whether all these crimes had truly happened and to make it clear to criminals that they would be held personally responsible for serious violations of humanitarian law. The Security Council reserved the right to take any measures it deemed appropriate, including the initiation of criminal trials, within six months. Everyone now agrees that justice is an immediate priority. It is the only hope for a solution to the human and humanitarian disaster which has spread to neighbouring countries.

Aware of the enormity of the task ahead, and at the request of the new government, the UN announced that it would send 20 investigators to determine who was responsible for the genocide and 145 international observers to deter individual acts of revenge. In reality, the UN hid for more than three months behind a single human rights observer based in Kigali: he had no car and no means of communicating with the outside world. Since then, no more has been said about the 145 observers. The arrival of three other investigators in September 1994 — who also lack the necessary resources to carry out their job effectively — has done nothing to improve this situation.

Justice or chaos

In light of the failure of the peacekeeping system, the UN is trying to revive the myth that is international justice. While the very notion of an international community is jeopardised by the collective abandonment of certain countries and peoples, the UN is looking for a new basis for peace in the world. Given the minimum rules for the exercise of state power, the UN's discourse on justice and the condemnation of criminals at international level are to be the cornerstones of this new international social contract. However, the insufficiency of the means employed by the UN to back up this rhetoric on justice ultimately fails to counter political chaos and impunity.

The evocation of justice has an immediately comforting effect on public opinion. It places a presentable shroud over the dead. It provides an epitaph for the anonymous victims of the massacres. UN justice functions like a funeral service which keeps a chastising flame burning above the empty chair of the unknown criminal.

But as the years go by, who will worry about the progress of the legal proceedings? Who will worry about the financing needed to ensure that truth be known about the dead, when there was no money to save them when they were still alive? And who will worry about justice for the dead, when it is the living who vote and who are the country's future?

Justice has slowly taken on an objective and rational form within individual countries. But at international level, it still resembles the medieval "wrath of God". Trial by politics is still the rule today and only History is the judge. Having realised that intervening between the warring parties is no solution to conflict, the UN has tried to find other ways to ensure a democratic, non-violent outcome to these situations. The organization of free elections was undertaken under UN surveillance to put an end to the conflicts in Cambodia, El Salvador, Mozambique, Angola and the western Sahara. However, election results can be quickly overturned when political adversaries remain armed. Worse yet, the need for political factions to control the largest part of the electorate prior to the holding of UN elections gives rise to a new type of organised violence:

— in Mozambique, the repatriation of refugees and their resettlement are not dictated by their own wishes. The mining and de-mining of roads and certain areas is the source of new outbreaks of fighting. It is no longer a matter of a military strategy for defending or controlling territory, but a political strategy for winning over the electorate;

— in Rwanda, the desire to retain control over the population led the fleeing government to organise the massive exodus of people. This seemingly democratic settlement of conflicts often amount to: one hostage, one vote. In this way political leaders vie for control of the electorate.

Unpunished crimes

For now, the main constraint on international law is that, with few exceptions, peace is won at the expense of justice. Justice is considered by politicians to be a luxury, a means of exerting pressure or issuing threats, a currency that can be exchanged against an imposed peace or a process of national reconciliation. For confirmation of this, we need only open a penal code to the section on war crimes: all we will find are laws on amnesty. Only the crimes of the Nazis were prosecuted on the basis of special legislation. The rule is too often confused with the exception when it comes to the showcase trials of former Nazis. Since 1950, impunity has been synonymous with stability in the realm of international policy. Any historical record of the creation of the international war crimes tribunal for former Yugoslavia will show that the main purpose of this body was not to try criminals. Created on 25 May 1993 by a Security Council resolution, it is presented as a peacekeeping measure. During 1994, the prospect of being brought to trial was meant to have a dissuasive effect on the pursuit of hostilities and to persuade the parties to sign peace agreements. However, the Security Council would wait more than a year before designating the prosecutor in charge of investigating the cases.

If there is any parallel with the Nuremberg trials, it is not to be found in terms of speed or effectiveness. It will take at least a year and a half for the UN to decide to set up the tribunal for former Yugoslavia, six months to appoint the judges, six more months to adopt a budget and rules of procedure, and an additional year to start the initial proceedings. By this time, the tribunal's budget will be spent and it will be necessary to hold new discussions for the adoption of a new budget. Finally, whether one is talking about its budget, its staff or the services made available to it by the states, the international tribunal will function under the surveillance of and be dependent upon the states.

In addition to these practical problems, the tribunal will not be able to ensure that justice be done for three outstanding reasons:
— it brings the victims who have lost everything face to face with the criminals who won, who have every possible means of putting pressure on and retaliating against witnesses and all possible means of falsifying or hiding material proof on site;
— because the scope of the task would oblige the tribunal to choose its cases: timeliness and impartiality would dictate the tribunal's choice of files to investigate, bringing all sides into question;
— finally, because the tribunal must respect the normal rules of the right to defence vis-à-vis the accused, which are applicable in all traditional legal proceedings, i.e., the presence of a lawyer, access to the facts of the case and cross-examination of witnesses. The accused will have the legal means of defending themselves and the illegal means of taking revenge, while the victims will receive no protection, will not have the assistance of legal counsel and will receive no compensation.

Nevertheless, the risks to the victims, the impediments to justice and all the disadvantages of such a tribunal must not obscure the tremendous revolution which the current discourse on international justice represents. After having attempted to keep peace at the expense of justice, there is now talk of rendering justice in order to achieve peace. This will bring into question the myth of the impunity of the victors. Force is being challenged by non-conventional weapons wielded in a closed arena with, on the one hand, those who have nothing to lose and, on the other, those who have gained everything and who may, in the long run, elude the political authorities.

Humanitarian law and justice

As we waver between cynicism and idealism, between the need to believe in justice and the desire not to be lulled by promises of a bright future, it is useful to go back to the sources of humanitarian law. Humanitarian law is not a dogma. It has always been on the front line between violence and survival. Thus, by nature, it covers both political and military contingencies. The difficult relationship between the just and the good is dealt with clearly and without the ambiguity heroism sometimes entails. In humanitarian law, justice is not a luxury but an indispensable guard against madness. This is not petty vengeance but the necessary act of repairing the torn social and human fabric, a check against the syndrome of violence begetting violence.

Today a debate is raging between those who believe that humanitarian action must provide care and comfort without addressing the root of the evil and those who believe that providing aid is only the beginning of humanitarian action. The first group points conveniently to the humanitarian tradition embodied by the International Red Cross. By hiding behind this kind of intellectual reference, they confuse impartiality with blindness.

The humanitarian principle of impartiality offers aid to victims without discrimination on the basis of political, ethnic or religious allegiance. In short, it obliges humanitarian agencies to care for any individual who is a victim and to close their eyes to the person's past. But closing one's eyes to the past of a victim does not mean being blind to the political, military and commercial diversion of aid meant for the victims. Neutrality cannot be interpreted as the right of political officials on both sides to receive equally lavish amounts of humanitarian aid.

Is not denouncing the diversion of humanitarian aid destined for civilians like denouncing the abuse of the Red Cross emblem? This abuse has a name in the Geneva Conventions: deceit. Since 1949, the military has learned many ways of abusing humanitarian law and, notably, aid going to civilians. This deceit must be denounced by those who claim to be reaching the victims and caring for those who are weakest.

During the preparatory work in codifying the Geneva Conventions, it was the signatories who felt it necessary to include not only the respect for the sick and wounded, but also the notion of severe sanctions for any serious infringements. Believing that high-sounding principles would not protect the victims, the signatories included in the four Geneva Conventions the three tools needed for a just use of force:

— they drew up a precise list of the most serious violations of the Conventions;

— they affirmed and defined the principle of the personal

responsibility of those who perpetrate infractions or who order these infractions;

— they invented a revolutionary and bold mechanism for sanctions: each state that is a party to the Conventions has the obligation to search for persons suspected of having committed or having ordered the commission of serious infractions, and the state must try these persons in its own courts, regardless of the perpetrator's nationality.

These Conventions have also provided two guarantees for this obligation to bring criminals to trial:

— a state cannot extradite a criminal to another country unless the person will be subject to punishment of equal severity. This is the only event in which the state itself is not obliged to try the accused;

— a state can never be exonerated from its responsibility to try the accused by adopting a law of amnesty or by signing international agreements (peace agreements) which provide impunity for crimes committed by both parties to a conflict.

The re-emergence at international level of the concepts of humanitarian law and justice will not put an end to war crimes. However, it will make a modest contribution — one that may soon become a reality. The invocation of law and justice at international level, even if done hypocritically, has undoubtedly contributed to increased awareness of the procedures of universal penal jurisdiction. Cases have been brought before a number of national courts this year by foreign victims as a result of the Geneva Conventions. In any event, the international justice that is emerging from the tribunal for former Yugoslavia in the Hague cannot flourish in the presence of the cowardice of the national justice systems.

9

ANTI-PERSONNEL MINES: THE WAR WITHOUT END

by Philippe Chabasse

In more than thirty countries, even in peacetime, anti-personnel mines indiscriminately kill and maim soldiers and civilians alike, women and children included. Uncontrolled mine-laying prevents civilians returning to a normal life and slows down the resettlement of refugees. In practice, it amounts to a scorched-earth policy.

The statistics speak for themselves. Although only rough estimates by western standards, they are no less horrendous for it: 25,000 amputees out of a population of 8 million in Cambodia; 20,000 to 30,000 out of Afghanistan's 12 million people; 20,000 out of 15 million in Angola

Under international law, the use of most of these mines is outlawed but it is evidently a dead letter situation. This scourge should be attacked at source, by demanding that the manufacture, sale and use of mines cease altogether.

An ongoing world crisis

Land mines, and in particular anti-personnel mines, are the favourite weapon in a dirty war campaign. Victims in the Third World are typically nomadic herdsmen and peasant families living off the land, with no way of escaping their fate or making the rest of the world aware of it. Mines are responsible for devastation in Afghanistan, Cambodia, Angola, Somalia, Ethiopia, Sudan, Uganda, Rwanda, Mozambique, Nicaragua, Laos, El Salvador, Vietnam, Iraq, Iran, Sri Lanka, Burma, Bosnia-Herzegovina... and the list goes on.

The following attests to the gravity of the situation whereby entire populations are decimated:

— in Cambodia, in 1994, mines have killed or maimed around 300 people a month;

— in the Plain of Jars, in Laos, 46 people were wounded and 23 killed in 1990 alone: seventeen years after the last mines were dropped by US warplanes, the danger is still there and the slaughter continues;

— in 1993, over a 10-month period, the hospital at Hargeisa in northern Somalia treated 147 land-mine victims, including 113 children under the age of 15;

— in 1989 and 1990, in the district of Spin Boldak in the Afghan province of Kandahar, 2 percent of the population were reportedly killed by mines and 3.5 percent injured;

— the hospital at Sulaymaniyah, in Iraqi Kurdistan, treated over 1,650 injuries from land mines between March and September 1991, including 398 requiring amputation.

An autonomous weapon

Invented and developed during the First and Second World Wars, anti-personnel mines were originally intended to protect strategic areas and installations for short periods. Their indiscriminate use is a relatively recent phenomenon: beginning with the US dropping of "bombies" over Laos up to 1973, it was only in the early 1980s, with the Soviet intervention in Afghanistan, that large-scale indiscriminate mine dispersal really took off. Once modern armies had discovered new uses for them, cheap anti-personnel mines were deployed on a massive scale, both by regular armies and by guerrilla movements, to prevent, channel or provoke civilian population movements.

Their widespread use does not fully explain the scale of the human carnage caused, however. The other sad feature of this weapon is that it fights on long after hostilities have ceased. Many potentially rich agricultural regions are threatened by land mines, and the danger grows as a population increase necessitates the cultivation of new land. The permanent nature of the threat, and the fact that land mines, once laid, are out of anyone's control, distinguishes them from all other weapons.

The objective of the soldier laying mines is to close off territory from the enemy. He primes the device so that the slightest pressure will cause it to explode... some time in the future. Once this is done, no one controls the weapon — neither the soldier, nor his superiors, nor anyone else can determine exactly what will happen. Even if a cease-fire is declared, each mine still retains its lethal potential, possibly for decades to come. This is no minor problem: the United Nations estimates that there are some 100 million live mines buried away in the soil of our planet. In Cambodia alone, there are reported to be 10 million.

If the order is given, it is possible to recover, neutralize or destroy them; the conventions governing the rules of warfare require minefields to be mapped. Unfortunately, in most cases the maps are simply non-existent — not just because the soldiers are negligent or ill-intentioned, but because of the very design of the mine and the strategy behind its use.

How, for example, does one map the position of mines designed to be scattered by the thousand from a plane or by artillery rounds (at a rate of up to 4,000 a minute)? In addition they are manufactured using materials deliberately selected to make them increasingly difficult to detect. Thus, the mine outlives the war, an autonomous weapon, waiting for its next victim.

The Falklands: sheep may safely graze ... some time after the year 2010?

◆

During the Falklands War, in 1982, the Argentine army laid mines all over the islands' beaches to prevent the expected British landings. The operation was conducted in strict accordance with international conventions, and the locations of the minefields were recorded quite precisely. Upon surrendering, the Argentine forces handed over the maps to their British counterparts.

Even with this kind of help, mine clearance costs time and human lives. Eager to return to more hospitable climes, the British army carefully filed the maps and went home.

In 1988, following a campaign in the UK, experts were appointed to clear the mined areas. But in the intervening six years, rain, snow and erosion had rendered the maps hopelessly out of date. The experts settled for fencing off the affected areas with mile upon mile of barbed wire.

The barbed wire is still there. There has been no campaign to count the three-legged sheep, a unique, living monument to non-compliance with international conventions.

In view of the scale and specific nature of the problem, there are three possible responses: humanitarian, technical and political. They all, to varying degrees, involve Non-Governmental Organizations (NGOs), military authorities, states and various UN bodies.

Humanitarian aid: only part of the answer

At first sight, the simplest way of responding is to provide humanitarian aid: giving the surgical facilities needed to save lives or at least, in an emergency, to be able to amputate limbs under the best possible conditions, and eventually supplying artificial limbs which will give the amputee the physical means to lead as normal a life as possible.

Looked at more closely though, the medical response has repercussions for the entire health and social security system, from first aid to vocational rehabilitation by way of ambulance services, surgical supplies, blood and drugs, physiotherapy, counselling, home help and community care. In addition to the individual human tragedies they cause, land mines wreak havoc on the fragile health systems of the countries affected. Now that reconstruction is beginning in Cambodia and Mozambique, for example, the priority should be to tackle the major diseases or train health workers, but the bulk of both local and international funds is devoted to looking after land mine victims.

Mine clearance: delays and false starts

Mine clearance represents a more preventive approach to the crisis. But large-scale de-mining is slow, costly and dangerous. Moreover, reclaiming land for domestic use after a conflict is an entirely new problem for the international community. No military doctrine covers it, no specific technique has yet been developed.

While armed forces know how to clear a way through a minefield in a conflict and can calculate an acceptable level of risk in doing so, civil mine clearance has to be 100 percent effective. The knowledge, or even suspicion, that there are land mines in a particular area prevents any civilian use of it. At present, the only technique which meets this criterion is manual mine clearance — using a metal detector and a bayonet — which enables the ground to be probed inch by inch.

The technical problems count for little in the general strategic muddle surrounding the few operations currently under way. In recent peace agreements (Cambodia, Mozambique, and Abkhazia, for example), mine clearance has merely been a way of facilitating the return of refugees, itself no more than a prelude to free elections. While it should have been considered as a matter of urgency on humanitarian grounds, mine clearance has often been used as a political football by the various local factions, UN bodies and the states sponsoring the peace agreements. More serious still, in addition to this general irresponsibility, no general conditions have been drawn up to establish minimum requirements for mine clearance operations (who, how, where, and at what cost?).

This absence of rules has led to anarchic competition between private mine clearance companies now thriving on the market. In Mozambique the UN secretly negotiated de-mining contracts with specialist companies owned by the major manufacturers of anti-personnel mines. In the light of such cynicism, inertia and scandals, increasing numbers of NGOs are acquiring or developing specialist skills in this field. This has the advantage, as in Cambodia where progress is being made, of actually getting things moving, but at the risk of letting the relevant institutions off the hook.

The hypocrisy of international conventions

The ultimate step in any preventive strategy is to tackle the production and sale of such weapons. At France's initiative, therefore, an international conference has been convened for 1995 to revise (i.e. strengthen) international law on the subject, namely the 1981 Convention on excessively injurious or indiscriminate weapons.

Although about ten countries have taken the first steps to ban the export of anti-personnel mines, their attempts to reform international law go no further than improving systems for controlling and imposing sanctions on their *use* only. Given that there is no way of controlling most of the warring parties concerned, it is fair to question the intellectual honesty of those who think they can solve the problem by restricting only the use of such weapons. In any case, it is the very design of the mine that determines its use (which is by definition indiscriminate) and the long-lasting nature of the threat it presents.

The development of so-called "smart" mines, which can be programmed over time, is another recipe for disaster. In addition to technical objections (the unreliability of such devices and disagreements between military planners on how long they should be programmed to last), developing such new technologies means making a distinction between those who can afford to pay the additional cost for such technology and those who cannot. Poor countries would surely ignore any international convention that banned them from using land mines while allowing the richest or most technologically advanced nations to use them.

There are therefore three potential drawbacks to this strategy: the international conference to reform the law could fail because of it; traditional mines could flood the market at low prices, and, in the field, "smart" mines could be used alongside traditional mines, thereby wiping out their theoretical advantages.

The only realistic solution has to be a total ban on the manufacture, storage, sale and use of all types of anti-personnel mines. That is what over sixty NGOs are demanding as part of an international campaign. The International Committee of the Red Cross (ICRC), the United Nations Children Fund (UNICEF), the United Nations High Commissioner for Refugees (UNHCR) and the UN Secretary General, Mr. Boutros Boutros-Ghali, have all expressed support for such a move.

Military double-think

Strangely enough, a growing number of military personnel come to the same conclusion, and — in private, or when confronted in the field with the fearful difficulties of mine clearance — recognize their responsibilities as professionals for what happens in the war zone when the conflict is over.

The main body of the armed forces, on the other hand, sees things differently and put the onus for post-conflict solutions squarely on the politicians — the same politicians who are conspicuous by their absence in international negotiations. The disturbing turn taken in the preparations for the 1995 conference demonstrates the inability of diplomatic and military experts to negotiate in the UN without a clear mandate from their political masters.

Any significant progress on the part of the international community will depend, in this as in many other issues, on the political will of the individual states concerned. Do Western leaders have the political courage to go all the way and move unilaterally towards banning the manufacture of anti-personnel mines? At stake are the lives and the limbs of thousands of innocent people for decades to come.

10

FOOD AID AND VITAMIN DEFICIENCIES IN THE REFUGEE CAMPS

by Erwann Queinnec and Jean Rigal

At the end of the 1980s the total number of refugees throughout the world stood at approximately 15 million and was virtually matched by the number of displaced persons forced by civil war to move within their own countries. The numbers grew to 19 million in 1993, and the exodus from Rwanda, in 1994, has swollen the ranks of the uprooted. One could be excused for believing that the end of the Cold War and East-West rivalry might have decreased the displacement of populations. Nothing could be further from the truth. Each year has brought another million refugees.

Protecting refugees outside the borders of their home country is part of the mandate of the Office of the United Nations High Commissioner for Refugees (UNHCR), which also acts as a co-ordinator of the relief organizations which volunteer their services to help such people. In the case of the world's 25 million displaced persons, however, access to outside help is hampered by a legal vacuum, national sovereignty and, above all, the danger generated by civil war.

The mortality rates recorded for the first weeks of any refugees' stay at a reception centre show how vulnerable the refugees are. The figures are seven to seventy times higher than they would be for a settled population. Rates of 5 to 10 deaths per 10,000 people per day are frequent. If they were projected beyond the initial period of emergency and continued at the rate of a disaster, they would be equivalent to 20 to 60 percent of the population dying in a year.

The main killers are measles, diarrhoea, respiratory infections and malaria, all easily controllable in a stable situation with basic medical equipment and treatment. Even more serious are problems of nutrition, as these provide the basis for most infectious diseases taking hold. Children under the age of five remain the most frequent victims of the food shortages caused by being forced to flee one's home. Surveys show malnutrition in these situations running at 20 to 50 percent and — significantly — going hand-in-hand with high mortality. Put in simple terms, a mild attack of malaria is enough to put the life of a severely malnourished child at risk.

2,000 kilocalories a day

The mandate of the World Food Programme (WFP) is to respond to host countries' requests for help in coping with immediate needs. Its member countries usually contribute goods, but may also donate money or services. The WFP usually arranges supplies to be shipped to a port or border in the country making the request, and will on occasion pay for delivery of supplies to the refugee camps. In rare cases, like "Operation Lifeline" in Sudan, it may monitor distribution on the ground itself. More often, the job of dealing with the logistics of getting the aid from the port to the refugee is performed by national Red Cross societies or Non-Governmental Organizations (NGOs) specializing in such activities. In recent years, the WFP and UNHCR have increased the number of joint evaluations and co-operation reports produced, not just in the case of programmes of assistance for refugees, but also for displaced persons (particularly in former Yugoslavia). This is done in the interests of more efficiency and speed in responding to needs in an emergency. Feeding refugees and displaced persons usually takes the form of distributing to each individual or family rations which have to provide approximately 2,000 kilocalories per person per day. They usually contain cereals (whole or in the form of flour), peas, beans or pulse, a small amount of oil and sometimes sugar. As an example, the theoretical daily ration received by Mozambican refugees in Malawi from the WFP and UNHCR is 400 grams of cornmeal, 60 grams of beans, 40 grams of oil, sugar and salt. This is an acceptably balanced mixture of food — fat, sugar and protein — vital for survival. When the numbers of refugees run into hundreds of thousands, mass distribution of such rations requires thousands of tonnes of supplies to be shipped and stored (often in inaccessible areas) and flawless logistics at every stage of distribution. It is not difficult to imagine the potential pitfalls. There may be a lack of money to pay for transport, funds may not have been budgeted or items in which there is a high stake in some parts of the world may just vanish (only to reappear in a private market). Every potential problem must be foreseen and will certainly have been encountered before. The victims of such problems are always the recipients. An example is provided by what happened in November and December 1993 in Burundian refugee camps in Rwanda and Tanzania, where the average food ration was between 300 and 800 kilocalories per person per day (depending on the camp). The disgrace was that the WFP stores in Kigali, no more than fifty kilometres away, were known to be full. Whether the cause was carelessness or theft, the estimated number of child deaths during this breakdown in food distribution was 9,000.

Vitamin deficiency on an epidemic scale

2,000 kilocalories a day is just enough to sustain life. Its monotony shows the discomfort of a refugee's circumstances. Even if he does eat, his troubles are not necessarily over. All too often, much more attention is paid to the quantity than to the quality of the food. This has been known to cause unexpected nutritional disaster.

Serious and widespread vitamin deficiencies have occurred in camps housing refugees and displaced persons during the last decade. Some of these instances could have been resurrected from the dark recesses of medicine's past. It was as if a human laboratory had been set up to recreate clinical situations which medical schools had forgotten existed. Vitamins are present in a balanced diet and are vital in small quantities to keep the body in working order.

Scurvy. — This disease, caused by vitamin deficiency, has become extremely rare in stable areas of the globe but has reappeared several times in recent years in the Horn of Africa. The vitamin lacking is vitamin C, usually obtained from fresh fruit and vegetables and (in the case of babies) from mother's milk. The clinical signs of scurvy are pain in the lower limbs, temporary paralysis and haemorrhage. Scurvy was recorded in camps housing Ethiopian refugees in Somalia (1982, 1985 and 1989), camps housing Ethiopian and Eritrean refugees in Sudan (1984 and 1991) and in camps housing

Somali refugees in Ethiopia (1989). In some camps it affected half the occupants.

Pregnant women are particularly at risk. The longer the stay in a refugee camp, the greater the risk of scurvy. Calculations have been made of the vitamin C content of some camps' rations: it is approximately 2mg per person. The level below which symptoms of deficiency begin to appear is 10mg.

The treatment for such a deficiency, in cases in which the victims run into the thousands, is mass distribution of ascorbic acid tablets, an undertaking which is a logistical nightmare. The best solution is to include fresh food in the usual ration or to supply vitamin C enriched flour.

Pellagra. — This disease has been known about since the 17th century but is now extremely rare except where there is multiple vitamin B and protein deficiency. Many cases are reported every year in India and eastern and southern Africa. It is caused by niacin (or vitamin PP) deficiency and is typified by dry skin lesions on areas of the body exposed to the sun. Later stages bring diarrhoea and problems with the central nervous system which can lead to cachexia resulting in death.

Over 22,000 cases were reported in 1989 and 18,000 cases in 1990 among the 900,000 Mozambican refugees in Malawi. The outbreaks arose because the camps had not been supplied with groundnuts between January and May 1989 and between January and July 1990. While this supply problem was tackled, the sick were treated with niacin tablets and vitamin B complex tablets were distributed as a preventive measure to all the occupants of the camps. As an experiment, enriched cornmeal was also distributed.

Beriberi. — This is largely a result of thiamine (vitamin B1) deficiency, but it often accompanies nutritional, protein or other B vitamin deficiencies. It is most common in South-East Asia among those whose diet consists mostly of milled rice. Public health measures in the countries of the area have made it less prevalent, but there were serious outbreaks in the refugee camps on Thailand's eastern border in 1985.

There are two clinical forms of beriberi in adults. Dry beriberi typically produces nervous symptoms which often begin by causing difficulty in walking and progress to paralysis. Wet (cardiovascular) beriberi produces heart problems. The two often occur together. Infantile cardiovascular beriberi can result in sudden heart failure even in an apparently well-fed child. Intravenous thiamine produces a dramatic improvement, but treatment with digitalis is ineffective.

Close examination of infant mortality figures for Karen refugees on the Thai side of the Burma-Thailand border revealed this disease. The health care system which has been in operation for years allows morbidity and mortality to be tracked. Malaria remains a major public health problem in the area, and a network of dispensaries with laboratory facilities and a system of proper patient treatment has been set up. It was noticed that infant mortality remained too high despite these measures. Closer examination of the causes of this abnormal rate revealed that many two- to four-month-olds in apparently good health were dying suddenly. They had suffered no fever, but had developed serious heart problems which failed to respond to symptomatic treatment. The automatic administration of intravenous thiamine in such cases after 1991 brought infant mortality down by half. An investigation of the dietary habits of lactating women revealed the source of the deficiency, and supplements were offered to the target group.

Xerophthalmia. — Vitamin A deficiencies causing xerophthalmia are common, widespread and not confined to refugees and displaced persons.

Vitamin A is found in fish liver oil, animal livers, eggs, cow's milk, palm oil and many fruits, but is almost completely missing from the rations distributed as international food aid.

Outbreaks of vitamin A deficiency usually strike children of pre-school age (one to five). They produce deteriorating night vision, damage to the cornea and blindness. Since vitamin A is also known to protect against diarrhoea, respiratory infections and measles, it follows that children with a deficiency are more likely to contract such complaints. Once a child is blinded by a vitamin A deficiency, he is usually considered to have a fifty-fifty chance of dying within six months.

Major occurrences appeared during the Ethiopian famine of 1984 and 1985, when groups of people already deficient in vitamin A moved from place to place and crossed borders. It is known that an adult's liver can provide enough vitamin A for six months, but this is not the case in children, who are the primary victims as a result. This shows the importance of supplements. It is also considered that once a group of displaced persons begins to show symptoms of vitamin A deficiency, it is living on nothing more than the body's reserves.

In such situations, it is customary to start blanket distribution of vitamin A tablets. This is of course a stopgap. It would be better to include a supplement in the basic food ration.

Listening to the refugees

It can be seen that the nutritional aid provided by international donors in emergency situations to displaced persons is often sufficient in terms of quantity but not quality. Vitamin deficiency on an epidemic scale is often not easy to detect. The key to prevention is to try to diversify the form of food aid (if possible while respecting the dietary habits of the recipients) and to enrich the flour distributed in the normal ration to prevent foreseeable deficiencies.

What is most important is to defend the refugee's freedom of movement, allowing him to change his diet, and to gear supplies to local resources. Efforts must be made to avoid the potentially dangerous monotony of international food aid. The right to freedom of movement is often rejected by the governments of the refugees' host countries, who fear creating a population imbalance and dealing with the political consequences of enormous flows of non-nationals. And yet there is potential gain for the host country in the money that can come through distributing aid to refugees.

It can be taken for granted in every refugee camp in the world that a hidden or not-so-hidden network of private markets will emerge within weeks of its opening. The better part of two weeks' worth of rations may end up being bartered for consumer goods which are considered more necessary. Some people think that these markets should be discouraged, arguing that selling food can lead to undernourished families. We should perhaps aim, when it becomes logistically possible, to provide considerably more than the 2,000 kilocalories per person per day that is the norm. This would allow people to exploit the market value of the small surplus they received. Nothing is simple, however, as the presence of international food aid sometimes undermines prices on local markets and thus harms local farmers.

It had sometimes been suggested that part or all of a food aid ration should be replaced by cash. While this has the merit of giving the refugees complete freedom, it has not often been tried, since its many detractors point out that it can cause suffering among the local people, who, if they are poor, may have standards of living no higher than the refugees themselves had before leaving their countries of origin. This plays down the hardship caused by being forced to move and rejects what might be a good solution when plentiful food is available close at hand.

Some refugees who have been in exile for years have been helped to set up fruit and vegetable patches (as in the case of Afghan refugees in south-western Pakistan) or provided with livestock (as in the case of several thousand Mozambican refugees in Zambia). Although hardly feasible in emergency situations, such initiatives deserve to be kept in mind. Land issues should never be forgotten in these instances, though. Many refugee communities are prohibited by their host countries from growing anything, and it is often the case that the land lent to the refugees is unsuitable for crops or grazing.

In conclusion, we should stress the importance of paying attention to good nutritional balance among those receiving international food aid, and that imagination and initiative must be exercised to introduce variety into their daily diet and above all to listen to their opinions and allow them to describe their needs.

11

TACKLING THE SOUTH'S MOST COMMON DISEASES

by Alain Moren

Of the 50 million deaths which occur in the world each year, 17 million are most probably caused by infectious or parasitic diseases. While these have little bearing on the mortality rates of the industrialized countries, where most deaths are related to chronic diseases, they are still the prime cause of death in the developing countries.

Measles, diarrhoea, acute respiratory infections and malaria are responsible for most deaths occurring in children under the age of five. Often aggravated by malnutrition, these diseases are responsible for what is called "avoidable mortality", i.e. deaths which could be prevented (through improved hygiene or vaccination) or effectively treated using inexpensive and easily accessible antibiotics. The majority of adult fatalities in developing countries are caused by tuberculosis. The tuberculosis endemic disease was revived by the AIDS epidemic at the beginning of the 1980s. All that it would take to control and prevent these infectious or parasitic diseases is easy access to care, diagnostic capacity, the availability of vaccines or treatment and the organization and financing of programmes run by qualified, paid personnel.

AIDS

Since the first AIDS cases appeared at the beginning of the 1980s the epidemic has known no bounds. It has spread across the world, taking a heavy toll on the African continent and, more recently, Asia, where it is now burgeoning. Recent estimates suggest 16 million people world-wide have been infected with the HIV virus, including 1 million children. In sub-Saharan Africa alone, over 10 million people have been infected since the beginning of the epidemic, with a further 2.5 million in Asia. All in all, over 2 million people have died of the disease since the end of the 1970s. There is still little prospect of an effective vaccine being developed in the near future, and progress in therapeutics has been slow despite the motivation of researchers.

Tuberculosis

Tuberculosis, a forgotten disease, long considered a thing of the past in the industrialized world, is on the increase again, partly because of the AIDS epidemic and the bacterium's increasing resistance to treatment. 8 million new cases of the disease and 3 million deaths world-wide are reported each year, making tuberculosis one of the biggest health concerns as the century draws to a close. It is the prime cause of death by infectious disease, and most of the victims are young adults, which means a considerable proportion of the active population of developing countries is being affected. As the fight against tuberculosis relies on diagnosis through laboratory examinations, poorer countries and areas inaccessible for economic or political reasons will have great difficulty in controlling the spread of the disease.

Although 95 percent of tuberculosis cases occur in the developing world, Europe and North America are also facing a renewed outbreak of the disease. The progress of the epidemic is affecting the entire world and we cannot hope to control its spread in a single region alone. The prevention and control of tuberculosis will depend on our ability to deal with the disease in the South. The threat of tuberculosis is now closely linked to the development of the AIDS epidemic, and the fact that the two aggravate each other is making the task even more difficult.

On paper, the treatment of tuberculosis is neither costly nor difficult. Modern techniques stop the infection and quickly make patients non-contagious. The problem is the minimum length of treatment (six months), which causes many sufferers in developing countries to give up before it is completed. The emergence of bacilli with a growing resistance to traditional forms of treatment makes it hard to control this endemic disease.

Yet solutions do exist and the necessary technology is available. However, the success of programmes to control tuberculosis will require major funding, along with the political will to develop new shorter forms of treatment and a more effective vaccine.

It is estimated that almost 88 million cases of tuberculosis will have occurred between 1990 and 1999, 8 million of them related to the AIDS epidemic. 30 million people will die of tuberculosis over the same period. Public health professionals and experts all agree that this renewed outbreak of (endemic) tuberculosis is not being dealt with properly at world level and that a major effort must be made to ensure that this low-profile disease becomes a priority once again in the eyes of potential donators and decision-makers.

Malaria

Malaria is another neglected disease of little interest to donators, if the funding difficulties encountered by most of the malaria control and research programmes are anything to go by. In 1990, some 90 countries world-wide were considered to be affected by malaria. More worrying still is the number of countries in the world (30 percent) in which the incidence of the disease, having once been controlled or stabilized, is currently changing or increasing significantly.

It is hard to put a figure on the number of malaria cases, though it is probably safe to say that there are between 300 and 500 million each year, over 90 percent of them in Africa. The total number of deaths caused by malaria could be as high as 3 million per year, including 1 million children under the age of five. Since 1957, *Plasmodium falciparum*, responsible for the most serious strain of malaria, has been developing a growing resistance to chloroquine, the main form of treatment for malaria since it was first used in 1934. This resistance was identified almost simultaneously in two outbreaks of the disease, in Colombia and on the border between Cambodia and Thailand, towards the end of the 1960s and spread rapidly, affecting Africa towards the end of the 1970s. The fear is that the same resistance might spread to all countries where *Plasmodium falciparum* is found.

Once various forms of resistance to chloroquine were observed, research teams began developing new forms of treatment, to which *Plasmodium* has once again become resistant. The treatment arsenal is rapidly running out of weapons and it will not be long before we see the first cases of malaria which resist all existing techniques. Such, at least, is the fear of most malaria experts. If strenuous research efforts are not made quickly, the disease will probably be associated once again with an extremely high rate of mortality. Research to come up with new forms of treatment and to develop a vaccine has often been described as timid and deserves to be supported in such a way that, as with tuberculosis, the disease is treated with the priority it deserves by the benefactors and governments of the industrialized countries.

The effective vaccine

It is estimated that 3 million infant deaths caused by measles, neonatal tetanus and whooping cough are avoided each year thanks to the vaccination programmes operating around the world. It is becoming ever more obvious that the vaccination of children is the most cost-effective way of operating in developing countries. Yet these diseases continue to cause 2 million deaths and 5 million cases of long-term effects every year.

After a period in which inoculation programmes speeded up and produced high levels of vaccination cover towards the end of the 1980s, there has been a worrying decline in figures since the beginning of the 1990s (see graph). This applies in particular to Africa. The sustained effort of the 1980s has slackened off since 1990. Vertical strategies are now being questioned and benefactors are altering their objectives and their methods of financing. On top of that has come the growing political and economic instability now affecting over half the countries of Africa.

The effort of the 1980s, seen as a success of the vaccination campaign, was based on the introduction of standard vaccination programmes and operations, applied in a set manner to all the developing countries with no margin for adjustment. The success, if success it was, tends to overshadow the fact that the results were very uneven and that a lot of countries are far from having achieved the vaccination-cover targets set under the world-wide child vaccination programme.

There is a growing realization that to maintain a high level of vaccination cover, we must adapt our tactics to take account of the varying standards attained by the health systems in different regions and countries. Many areas, especially in Africa, have become difficult to reach and so require imaginative approaches (because of the presence of displaced persons and deprived areas around towns). The vaccine distribution systems of the 1980s are unable to meet the requirements of the 1990s and need to be upgraded.

In the years ahead we can expect to see the appearance on the market of new vaccines developed for twenty or so major infectious diseases. The high cost of these vaccines produced using the latest technology is already a cause for concern. The pharmaceutical

WORLD VACCINATION COVERAGE FOR CHILDREN OF LESS
THAN ONE YEAR OF AGE. 1977-1993

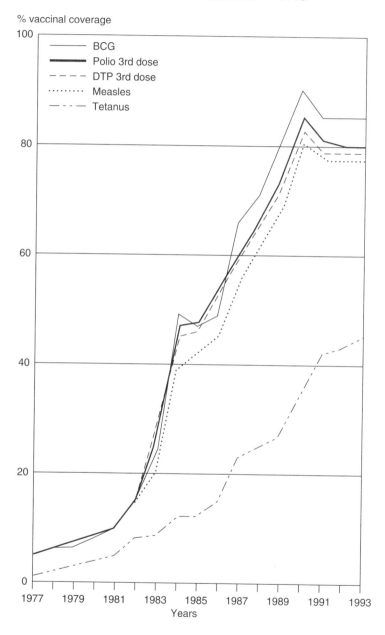

Source: World Health Organization; EVP.

industry's overriding need for profit means that production will be geared primarily towards industrialized countries. The existing cheaper vaccines might no longer be produced or available, which would deprive developing countries of a powerful tool against the infectious diseases responsible for a significant proportion of their infant mortality.

Current vaccination policies give a prominent place to diseases such as polio, yet eradication targets defined at a world level might well direct financial resources towards those countries where the chances of eradicating these diseases are greatest, at the expense of the poorest countries and areas where there is conflict or political instability, thereby accentuating their backwardness in health matters. Over the last ten years, vaccination programmes have proceeded under banners such as "Health for all in the year 2000" and "Universal vaccination in 1990", etc. Although these slogans have served to rally donors and governments behind the programmes' objectives, they may also have caused disappointment among health workers in the most disadvantaged countries, who had no hope of achieving or maintaining the objectives set by the international organizations. Those in charge of vaccination programmes thus became faithful implementers of programmes devised elsewhere, without the slightest scope for adapting them to the particular features of their country. International policies are now changing and will probably confuse health professionals.

For instance, the practice of opening multi-dose vaccine phials to inject a single child was recommended during the rich years of the 1980s. The current recession is forcing us to save on vaccines and cut out all wastage from programmes. The apparent success of the 1980s was short-lived. Unless the international community is willing to back research into new vaccines and make them available at affordable prices, and to come up with strategies which take account of the political instability now affecting many countries, deaths caused by diseases such as measles, whooping cough and tetanus will probably be on the increase by the end of the century.

Infectious and parasitic diseases are still a priority in developing countries, and some of them (measles, malaria, tuberculosis) are likely to flare up again unless the governments of the industrialized countries are prepared to act quickly and show the political and financial will to give new impetus and support to research and operations to prevent and treat each of these killers.

III

Humanitarian atlas

This humanitarian atlas presents a synthetic analysis of the principal problems faced by humanitarian organizations: conflicts, refugees, famines, epidemics. Each of these themes is introduced by planispheres which present a global vision of the world situation. Each individual theme is then further explored by a series of maps presenting a regional case study (conflict in Afghanistan, refugee movements in former Yugoslavia, famine in Angola, epidemics in Tajikistan). Finally, the last chapter is devoted to the particularly dramatic case of Sudan, where the four themes are united and their interconnection analysed.

◆

12

CIVILIANS
IN THE WAR ZONES

With regard to the ever-multiplying number of political crises, a certain confusion emerges. A distinction must be made between conflicts, instability and political violence and repression. A *conflict* implies a situation in which two groups opposed by incompatible interests or objectives are engaged in armed struggles in order to dominate, supplant or annihilate the other by force.

The apparent complexity of conflicts in turn gives rise to confusion about what is at issue in the combat. In Afghanistan, for example, the disappearance of ideological forces paved the way to an ethnic interpretation of the war. However, the issues of new or continuing conflicts demonstrate a certain uniformity. They involve the following: power conflicts, territorial conflicts, minority conflicts and separatist conflicts.

— *Power conflict:* a struggle between two groups in the same nation or between a group and the government. Power conflicts essentially are about exclusive access to or greater participation in political power. They often reflect the will of each party to dominate the other by totally or partially excluding it from power.

— *Territorial conflict:* a struggle between two groups in the same nation or two nations (whether or not they are represented by a state). Territorial conflicts concern the exclusive control of a territory and its resources. Each party is determined to oust the other, partially or totally, from the territory.

— *Minority conflict:* a struggle pitting a majority group or a government against an ethnic, linguistic or religious minority group. The principal issue is the recognition or tolerance of the specific identity of the minority. This is manifested notably by the refusal of the majority group to recognise the rights of the minority and its will to assimilate, suppress or expel the minority group from the territory.

— *Separatist conflict:* an armed struggle by a group or a nation for autonomy or political independence from a nation or state opposing this aim. This type of conflict often constitutes an exacerbated form of territorial conflict, power conflict or minority conflict.

While the issues of conflicts have been remarkably stable over a lengthy period, they increasingly affect civilian populations. Most present-day conflicts take place within the frontiers of a single country and increasingly in the midst of inhabited regions. As in the case of Afghanistan, civilian populations are directly exposed to fighting which indiscriminately attains military or civilian targets. They are sometimes even directly targeted by the combatants.

Moreover, while the issues of conflicts remain constant, their motivating forces evolve. The disappearance of the ideological cement has favoured the resurgence of long-standing antagonism and the multiplication of identity-related or nationalist demands. Torn by these divisions, populations are often involved in conflicts in which they represent the principal stake.

The end of the Cold War has also changed the economics of conflicts. Previously supported by the major powers, armed forces, guerilla fighters and states have had to find other means of financing their struggles, retaining power and assuring their survival. To do so, they do not hesitate to turn to civilian populations or humanitarian organizations, which they pillage, exact ransom from or take hostage. Civilian victims of conflict can now be distinguished as follows:

— *target population:* a population in immediate danger because it constitutes a stake in the conflict and is directly targeted by the protagonists: massacre, ethnic cleansing, deliberate famine or forced displacement of populations;

— *threatened population:* a population potentially in danger because it is trapped by the conflict: various deprivations, no access to care, looting and ransom, population movements, isolation, indiscriminate attacks;

— *vulnerable population:* a population weakened by the consequences of conflict on food provisions and health care, while its survival is not under imminent threat: refugees, shortages related to interrupted supplies (embargoes) or a drop in harvests, apartheid, difficult access to health care.

130

POWER CONFLICTS

1. Afghanistan: combat between factions following the withdrawal of the Red Army in February 1989; 3.4 million refugees.

2. Algeria: terrorism by Islamic groups since 1992.

3. Angola: resumption of conflict between the government (MPLA) and opposition forces (UNITA) since 1992; 325,000 refugees.

4. Cambodia: guerilla warfare between the Khmers Rouges and the government; 7,700 refugees.

5. Djibouti: confrontations between government troops (Issa) and the FRUD (Afar) opposition since 1991.

6. Ghana: February 1994, Nanumba/Konkomba confrontations.

7. Iraq (Kurdistan): PUK/KDP confrontations in May 1994.

8. Liberia: inter-factional conflicts since 1990; 700,000 refugees.

9. Peru: terrorism by Shining Path since 1980.

10. Rwanda: armed conflict between government and RPF forces since 1990; 730,000 refugees.

11. Sierra Leone: confrontations between government forces and the RUF since May 1991; 310,000 refugees.

12. Somalia: inter-factional conflicts since 1988; 517,000 refugees.

13. Chad (south): confrontations between CSNPD (Southern) forces and the government since 1992; 213,000 refugees.

14. Tajikistan: conflicts between the government and opposition forces since 1992; 13,300 refugees.

15. Yemen: armed confrontations during the attempted secession of ex-South Yemen in the spring of 1994.

TERRITORIAL CONFLICTS

16. Bosnia-Herzegovina: conflict between the Bosnian Serb forces and Bosnian and Croat forces since April 1992; 1.2 million refugees.

CONFLICTS AND POPULATIONS IN DA▮

17. Croatia: conflict between Croats and Serbs since 1991; 280,000 refugees.

18. Southern Lebanon: conflict between Israeli and Hezbollah forces since 1988.

MINORITY CONFLICTS

19. Bangladesh (Chakma): clashes between the majority Muslim population and Buddhist Chakmas since 1971; 56,000 refugees.

20. Burma: conflicts between the SLORC junta and Karen, Karenni, Mon, Wa and Shan guerilla fighters since 1948; 273,000 refugees.

21. India (Assam): confrontations between government forces and Assamese rebel movements since the 1950s.

22. Iraq: government repression/ opposing Chiites in the marshland.

JARY-AUGUST 1994)

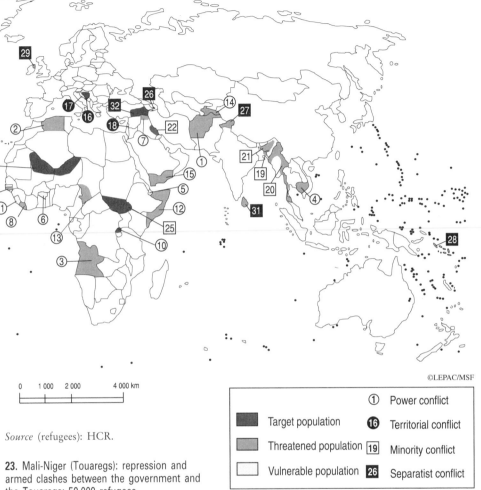

©LEPAC/MSF

Target population	① Power conflict
Threatened population	⑯ Territorial conflict
Vulnerable population	⑲ Minority conflict
	㉖ Separatist conflict

0   1 000   2 000   4 000 km

Source (refugees): HCR.

23. Mali-Niger (Touaregs): repression and armed clashes between the government and the Touaregs; 50,000 refugees.

24. Mexico (Chiapas): armed confrontations between the Mexican army and the Zapatist movement in early 1994.

25. Sudan (south): conflict between the government and the SPLA since 1983; 380,000 refugees.

SEPARATIST CONFLICTS

26. Azerbaijan (Nagorno-Karabakh): war between Azeri and Armenian separatists since 1988; 330,000 refugees.

27. India (Kashmir): confrontations between Indian forces and Muslim Kashmir separatists since 1990; 330,000 refugees.

28. Papua-New Guinea (Bougainville): guerilla war between the government and Bouganvillean separatists since 1989.

29. United Kingdom (Northern Ireland): conflict between unionists and separatists since 1969.

30. Senegal (Casamanca): confrontations between government forces and Casamancan separatists since 1982.

31. Sri Lanka (Tamuls): guerilla warfare between the government and Tamul separatists (LTTE) since 1977; 76,000 refugees in India.

32. Turkey (Kurdistan): conflict between Turkish government and Kurd (PKK) separatists.

Some of the solutions to conflicts

In view of the growing number of conflicts, the international community is increasingly called upon to try to provide solutions. It has a full range of instruments for this purpose, from economic sanctions to military intervention or peacekeeping operations:

— *Economic sanctions* (from embargoes to blockades): a binding measure taken by the Security Council against a country, prohibiting states from exporting and/or importing one or more products to the country.

— *Peacekeeping operations*: following a decision by the UN Security Council and with the agreement of the combatants, the deployment of observers or neutral intervention forces whose mission is fixed by mandate. Peacekeeping operations are only authorised to use force as a last resort and solely in cases of legitimate defence. There are two types of peacekeeping operations:

• observer missions: interventions with a mandate to observe compliance with a cease-fire or truces signed by the protagonists; the holding of orderly elections; military movements in zones of tension or protected areas;

• peacekeeping missions: in the first wave of interventions, the interposition of UN troops between the belligerent parties. Today, peacekeeping mandates are increasing in their scope. Such missions can play an active role in mine-clearance, the organization of elections, the demobilization and disarmament of combatants, the repatriation and reintegration of refugees, police training, the defence of human rights and the rebuilding of the economy.

— *"Humanitarian interventions"*: following a decision by the UN Security Council, the deployment of international troops whose mission it is to protect civilian populations or rescue operations and to restore security. In accordance with Chapter 7 of the UN Charter, these troops may intervene without the agreement of the combatants and are authorised to use force if necessary to accomplish their mission. In practice, however, they have carried out only so-called "humanitarian" missions. Indeed, the end of ideological confrontations has led the Security Council to adopt new intervention criteria. Essentially defined in accordance with moral values, they now lead states to intervene militarily in order to provide a humanitarian response to political conflicts. However, these operations remain limited and hardly manage to conceal governments' lack of will or political vision.

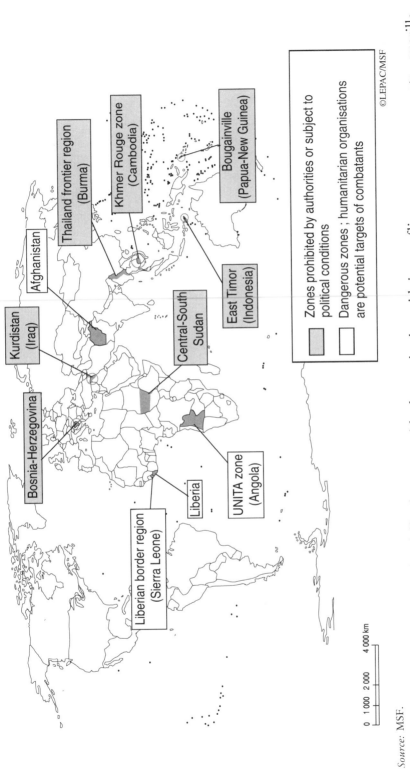

Afghanistan

Thailand frontier region
(Burma)

Khmer Rouge zone
(Cambodia)

Bougainville
(Papua-New Guinea)

East Timor
(Indonesia)

Kurdistan
(Iraq)

Central-South
Sudan

Bosnia-Herzegovina

Liberian border region
(Sierra Leone)

Liberia

UNITA zone
(Angola)

Zones prohibited by authorities or subject to
political conditions

Dangerous zones ; humanitarian organisations
are potential targets of combatants

©LEPAC/MSF

0 1 000 2 000   4 000 km

Source: MSF.

It is becoming increasingly difficult to provide humanitarian aid in conflict areas: governments, guerilla
movements and local authorities do not hesitate to prohibit or haggle over access to threatened populations.

COUNTRIES UNDER UNITED NATIONS EMBARGOES (AUGUST 1994)

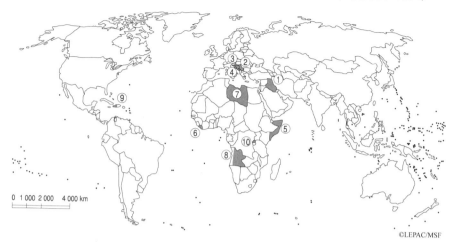

©LEPAC/MSF

Source: UN.

1. Iraq (1990): military, air (partial), technical, financial and trade embargo with the exception of food and essential medical products.

2. Serbia-Montenegro (1992/93): total embargo except on humanitarian aid.

3. Croatia (1991): arms embargo and total embargo on declared safe areas controlled by Serbian forces (except humanitarian aid).

4. Bosnia-Herzegovina: same as Croatia.

5. Somalia (1992): arms embargo.

6. Liberia (1992): arms embargo except for ECOMOG.

7. Libya (1993): air and military embargo and embargo on petroleum drilling and transport material; foreign assets frozen.

8. Angola (1993): arms embargo applied to UNITA.

9. Haiti (1994): total embargo.

10. Rwanda (1994): arms embargo.

UNITED NATIONS OPERATIONS (AUGUST 1994)

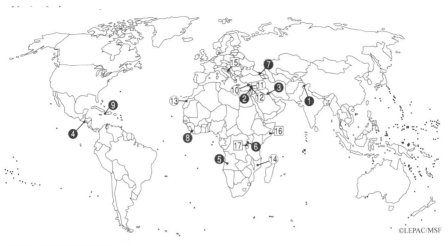

©LEPAC/MSF

- **①** Observation mission
- **⑩** Peace-keeping mission
- **15** "Humanitarian intervention"

0 1 000 2 000   4 000 km

Source: UN.

OBSERVATION MISSIONS

1. UNMOGIP (1948): observer group on the India/Pakistan frontier; observation of cease-fire; 40 men.

2. UNTSO (1948): truce surveillance in Palestine, Israel, Jordan, Lebanon, Syria and Egypt; 218 men.

3. UNIKOM (1991): observation mission on the Iraq/Kuwait border; 1,147 men.

4. ONUSAL (1991): observation group in El Salvador; monitoring of implementation of agreements between the government and guerilla troops; 250 men.

5. UNAVEM II (1992): verification mission in Angola; implementation of peace process; 77 men.

6. UNOMUR (1993): observation mission on the Ugandan/Rwandan frontier; 80 men.

7. UNOMIG (1993): observation mission in Georgia; 21 men.

8. UNOMIL (1993): observation mission in Liberia; 370 men.

9. UNMIH (1993): observation mission in Haiti (temporarily withdrawn).

PEACE-MAKING MISSIONS

10. UNFICYP (1964): force responsible for peacekeeping in Cyprus; monitoring of cease-fire; 1,218 men.

11. UNDOF (1974): force responsible for observing disengagement in the Golan Heights; monitoring of cease-fire since 1974; 1,033 men.

12. UNIFIL (1978): interim force in Lebanon, confirmation of Israeli withdrawal and restoration of peace; 5,231 men.

13. MINURSO (1991): mission for the referendum in western Sahara, responsible for electoral rolls; 310 men.

14. ONUMOZ (1992): operation in Mozambique; monitoring of cease-fire and co-ordination of humanitarian action; 5,929 men.

"HUMANITARIAN INTERVENTIONS"

15. UNPROFOR (1992): protection force in former Yugoslavia; 34,490 men.

16. UNOSOM II (1993): operation in Somalia to restore conditions of safety, democracy and economic re-organisation; 18,952 men.

17. UNAMIR (1994): assistance mission in Rwanda; 3,764 men.

THE AFGHAN CONFLICT

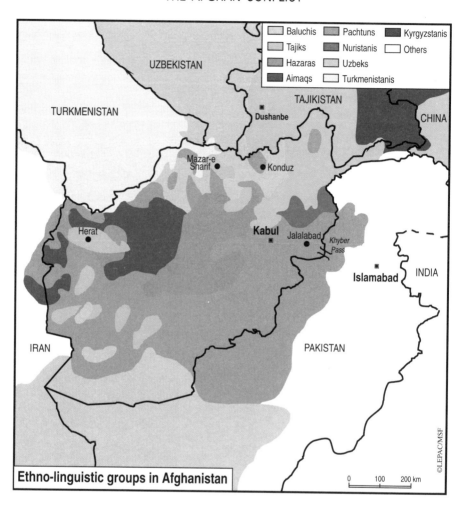

Ethno-linguistic groups in Afghanistan

©LEPAC/MSF

0   100   200 km

The map of the populations of Afghanistan shows the internal fragmentation of its territory and the country's ethnic ties with its Tajik, Uzbek and especially Pachtun neighbours. However, traditional territorial settlements have not been altered by 15 years of conflict. Indeed, the fighting is not aimed at any community in particular. Nor is any community spared, because the war in Afghanistan has resulted in more victims among civilians than among the combatants.

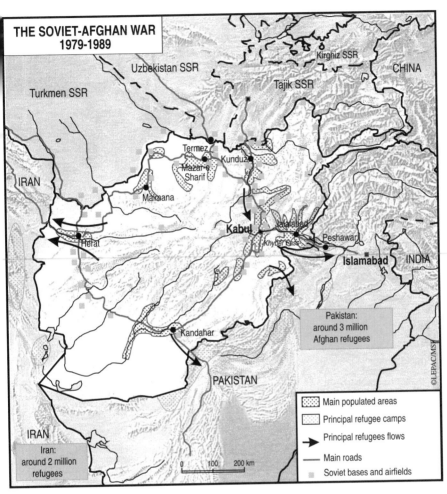

Source: HCR.

In December 1979, Afghanistan was invaded by Soviet troops. After ensuring their control of the towns, the troops attempted to stop the nascent resistance movements. The Soviets deployed their forces into populated areas for this reason. They tried to cut off the resistance from its rear base in Pakistan, laid millions of anti-personnel mines and installed bases along the circular route and the south-north main route linking Kabul to the USSR. More than one quarter of the Afghan population has fled the country.

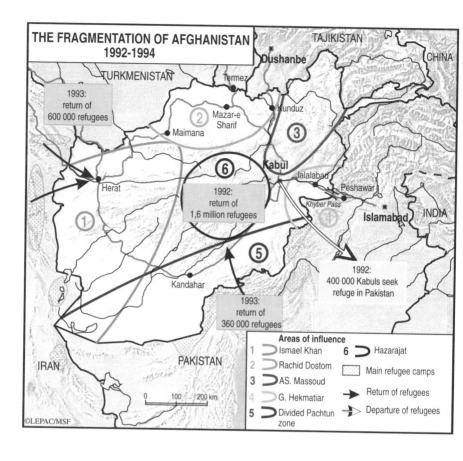

THE FRAGMENTATION OF AFGHANISTAN
1992-1994

TAJIKISTAN

CHINA

Dushanbe

TURKMENISTAN

Termez

1993:
return of
600 000 refugees

② Mazar-e
Sharif
Maimana

Kunduz

③

⑥ Kabul

Herat

1992:
return of
1,6 million refugees

Jalalabad

Peshawar

Khyber Pass

④

Islamabad

INDIA

①

⑤

Kandahar

1993:
return of
360 000 refugees

1992:
400 000 Kabuls seek
refuge in Pakistan

IRAN

PAKISTAN

0   100   200 km

©LEPAC/MSF

Areas of influence

1 ▷ Ismael Khan   6 ▷ Hazarajat

2 ▷ Rachid Dostom   ▢ Main refugee camps

3 ▷ AS. Massoud   → Return of refugees

4 ▷ G. Hekmatiar   ⇒ Departure of refugees

5 ▷ Divided Pachtun
zone

In 1989, the Soviets withdrew from Afghanistan. The victorious resistance movements fought over power and territories and divided the country into areas of influence, which relate only partially to existing ethnic groups. These zones of influence converge towards the capital, which has come to symbolise the power vacuum.

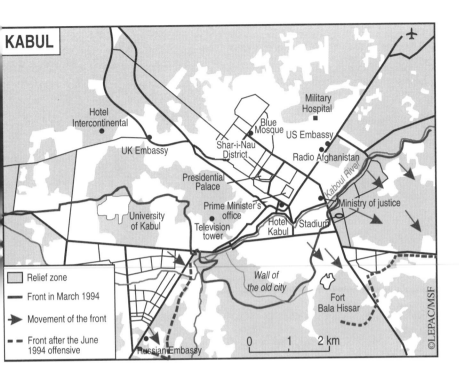

From 1989 to 1994, the conflict moved from the countryside to the cities and Kabul was cut in two by a moving front. While the restoration of peace to rural areas enabled numerous refugees to return home, the fighting in Kabul once again forced the population to flee the capital.

13

REFUGEES AND DISPLACED PERSONS THROUGHOUT THE WORLD

The Convention of 1951 defines a refugee as any person, "owing to well-founded fear of being persecuted for reasons of race, religion, nationality, membership of particular social group or political opinion, is outside the country of his nationality and is unable to or, owing to such fear, is unwilling to avail himself of the protection of that country (...)". This definition, which is centred around individual cases of persecution, reflects the post-war situation where most refugees were fleeing totalitarian regimes. These refugees were granted asylum in democratic countries where they benefited from a legal status and where they had rights resembling those of the citizens of the country in question.

Since then, the situation has changed greatly and the definition of a refugee has, in fact, been extended to include not only persecuted individuals, but groups of people who have been victims of violence. The numerous refugee movements of the last twenty years have, in fact, been more often linked to war, massive repression and famine than to individual persecution. Refugees are now fleeing collectively to neighbouring countries where they are grouped together in border camps and receive assistance and protection.

The end of the Cold War and the rapid increase in the number of asylum seekers in Western countries have led the international community to attempt to find "lasting solutions" to ever-increasing movements of refugees. The international community now seeks to prevent such movements, by providing humanitarian assistance inside the countries in crisis and by closing refugee camps, wherever possible, in order to encourage the repatriation of refugees to their regions of origin.

Finally, the definition laid down in the 1951 Convention does not apply to displaced people, who, like refugees, flee insecurity. Following the definition, persecuted individuals who do not cross national borders are not eligible for international protection. Left to fend for themselves, displaced people are unable to expect

142

Source: HCR.

Figures for December 1993, with the exception of Burundi, Rwanda and Zaire (figures for August 1994).

anything other than random assistance, depending on the access of humanitarian organizations.

Owing to the lack of reliable, detailed information on the subject, this chapter does not refer to displaced people, who number somewhere between 20 and 30 million.

RIGIN

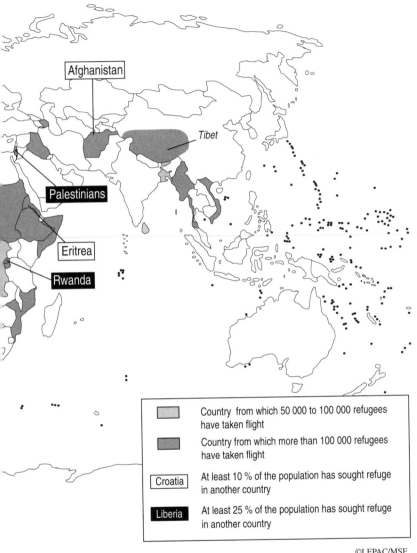

Afghanistan

Tibet

Palestinians

Eritrea

Rwanda

	Country from which 50 000 to 100 000 refugees have taken flight
	Country from which more than 100 000 refugees have taken flight
Croatia	At least 10 % of the population has sought refuge in another country
Liberia	At least 25 % of the population has sought refuge in another country

©LEPAC/MSF

Croatia

Guinea

0   1 000   2 000   4 000 km

Source: HCR.

Figures for December 1993, with the exception of Burundi, Rwanda and Zaire (figures for August 1994).

GEES WORLD-WIDE

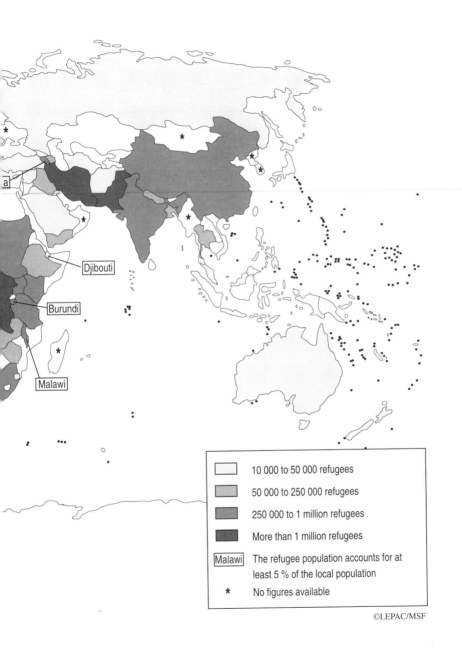

	10 000 to 50 000 refugees
	50 000 to 250 000 refugees
	250 000 to 1 million refugees
	More than 1 million refugees
Malawi	The refugee population accounts for at least 5 % of the local population
*	No figures available

©LEPAC/MSF

146

CONFLICTS, DISPLACED PERSONS AND REFUGEES IN FORMER YUGOSLAVIA (SITUATION IN AUGUST 1991)

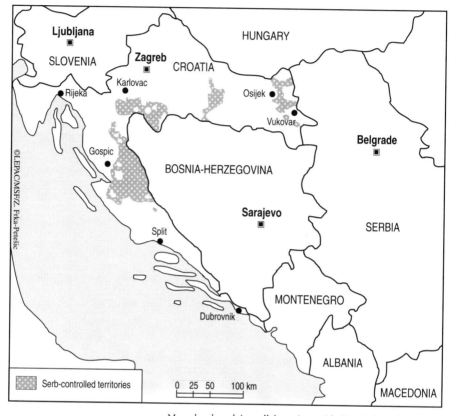

Map developed in collaboration with Zvonimir Frka-Petešic.

June 1991: fighting begins in Croatia.

25 June 1991: Croatia declares its independence.

23 August 1991: the ICRC announces that there are 90,000 displaced persons in Croatia.

October 1991: the US Committee for Refugees announces that there are more than 300,000 displaced persons in Croatia and 134,000 Serb refugees from Croatia in Serbia.

19 November 1991: besieged since the end of August by the Serbs, Vukovar falls. Before the war, the city had 56,000 inhabitants; during the siege, it was inhabited by 15,000 persons. In mid-November, an estimated 2,000 civilians and between 2,000 and 2,500 combatants have been killed in the city, now destroyed.

23 December 1991: Germany recognises Croatia.

15 January 1992: the EEC recognises Croatia.

3 February 1992: Croat President Franjo Tudjman "unconditionally" accepts the UN peace plan.

22 May 1992: Croatia is admitted to the UN.

February 1992: according to the HCR, there are 600,000 persons from Croatia who have been displaced or are refugees inside or outside the former Yugoslavia.

CONFLICTS, DISPLACED PERSONS AND REFUGEES IN FORMER YUGOSLAVIA (SITUATION IN JUNE 1992).

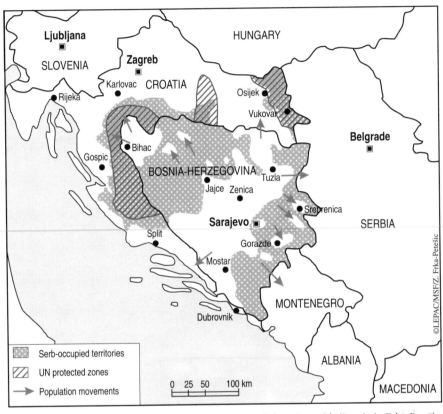

Map developed in collaboration with Zvonimir Frkà-Petešic.

March-April 1992: fighting begins in Bosnia-Herzegovina.

6 April 1992: the EEC recognises Bosnia-Herzegovina.

7 April 1992: Serb members of the Parliament of Sarajevo proclaim the independence of the Serbian Republic of Bosnia-Herzegovina.

22 May 1992: Bosnia-Herzegovina is admitted to the UN.

In mid-June 1992, around 380,000 persons are under siege in Sarajevo (450,000 including the outskirts). During the first week of June, the Serbs withdraw from the airport, making it possible in early July to establish an air lift for delivering humanitarian aid to the Bosnian capital.

In July 1992, the HCR reports that:
— 100,000 civilians are under siege in Tuzla;
— 250,000 to 300,000 in Bihac (the city had 70,900 inhabitants before the war);

— 65,000 to 70,000 in Gorazde (37,500 inhabitants before the war).

During the summer of 1992, the existence of Serb prison camps in Bosnia-Herzegovina is confirmed by the ICRC. They are one of the means used by the Serbs for ethnic cleansing; roughly 100,000 men are detained. The ICRC, which inspects the camps in August, denounces the "inhumane treatment" in the camps and the "massive and forced population transfers".

On 10 July 1992, HCR estimates the number of displaced persons and refugees in former Yugoslavia at 1,752,000, of which:
— 267,000 displaced persons in Croatia;
— 340,000 refugees from Croatia in former Yugoslavia;
— 500,000 displaced persons in Bosnia-Herzegovina;
— 945,000 refugees from Bosnia-Herzegovina in former Yugoslavia.

CONFLICTS, DISPLACED PERSONS AND REFUGEES IN FORMER YUGOSLAVIA (MARCH-APRIL 1993)

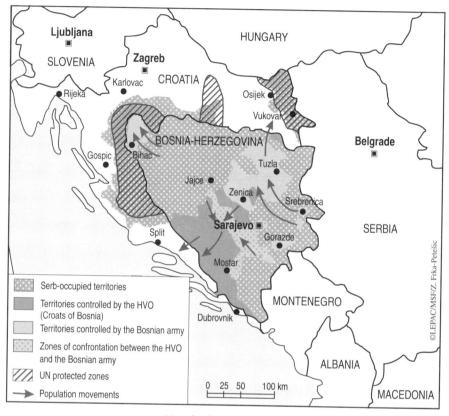

Map developed in collaboration with Zvonimir Frka-Petešić.

21 January 1993: Amnesty International publishes a report on the "systematic and organised" use of rape by Serb soldiers.

Spring 1993: fighting begins in central and southern Bosnia between the HVO (Croats of Bosnia) and the Bosnian army.

April 1993: UN Security Council Resolution 819 declares Srebrenica a "safe area". Resolution 824 creates five other "safe areas" : Sarajevo, Tuzla, Zepa, Gorazde and Bihac.

20 April 1993: the Serbs of Croatia and Bosnia announce their unification.

Spring 1993: the HCR estimates that there are 18,000 persons under siege in Zepa and around 50,000 in Srebrenica.

May 1993: the HCR counts a total of 2,280,000 refugees and displaced persons in Bosnia-Herzegovina.

CONFLICTS, REFUGEES AND DISPLACED PERSONS
IN FORMER YUGOSLAVIA (SITUATION IN THE SUMMER OF 1994)

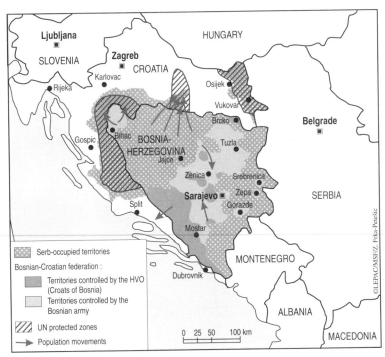

Map developed in collaboration with Zvonimir Frka-Petešic.

5 February 1994: a Serb shell kills 68 and wounds 300 at a Sarajevo market.
March 1994: the Croats and Muslims of Bosnia announce their agreement to form a federation in Bosnia.
29 March 1994: Serb offensive on Gorazde.
23 April 1994: the Serbs draw back after the NATO ultimatum. The Serbian offensive on Gorazde results in 436 dead and 1,467 wounded.

August 1994: the HCR counts 3,749,000 refugees and displaced persons in former Yugoslavia, of which:
— 2,775,000 in Bosnia-Herzegovina;
— 477,000 in Croatia;
— 405,000 in Serbia.

14

FAMINE
AND MALNUTRITION
WORLDWIDE

Famine is rare, confined to a certain area, temporary and always predictable. However, each year there are more victims of malnutrition than of famine. A distinction must be drawn between chronic malnutrition, food shortages and famine:

— *chronic malnutrition*: a set of symptoms linked to insufficient or imbalanced food intake, in particular among destitute populations. Malnutrition is generally characterised by slow growth, anaemia, greater vulnerability to disease and high infant and child mortality;

— *food shortages*: a temporary or local lack of certain essential foodstuffs related to : poor harvests, natural catastrophes, an interruption of imports or distribution, a sudden increase in demand due to massive population movements. In the most serious cases, shortage turns into scarcity and leads to the development or aggravation of malnutrition in the most vulnerable populations;

— *famine*: a localised, exceptional food emergency situation, characterised by a sudden rise in mortality. In famine situations death can be caused by different factors: acute malnutrition characterised by emaciation ("marasmus") or the appearance of generalised oedema ("kwashiorkor"); the weakening of the immune system, resulting in increased vulnerability to diseases caused by viruses, bacteria or parasites (measles, respiratory infections, diarrhoea).

0 1 000 2 000   4 000 km

Sources: MSF; FAO; World Bank.

DWIDE

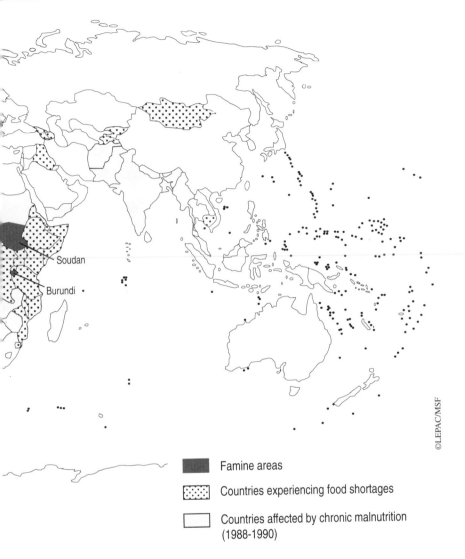

Soudan

Burundi ·

©LEPAC/MSF

Famine areas

Countries experiencing food shortages

Countries affected by chronic malnutrition
(1988-1990)

RISKS OF FAMINE IN AFRICA

A famine situation is always exceptional but never unexpected. It is the result of a combination of one or more of the following factors: drought, political crisis or conflict and the ensuing consequences such as the interruption of trade flows, social destruction and the displacement of populations.

The outbreak of famine and its scope are determined by the speed at which the alert is raised, the swiftness and scale of rescue efforts.

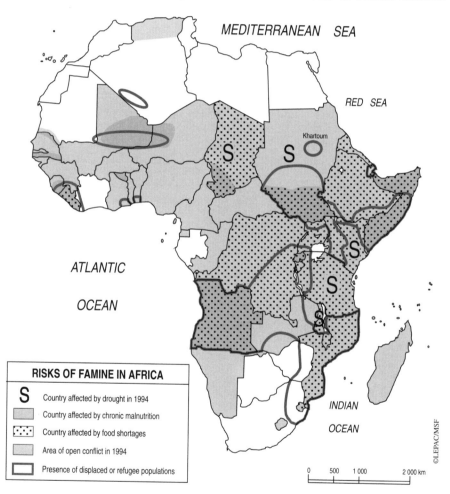

MEDITERRANEAN SEA

RED SEA

Khartoum

S   S

S

S

ATLANTIC

OCEAN

INDIAN

OCEAN

©LEPAC/MSF

RISKS OF FAMINE IN AFRICA

S	Country affected by drought in 1994
	Country affected by chronic malnutrition
	Country affected by food shortages
	Area of open conflict in 1994
	Presence of displaced or refugee populations

0   500   1 000   2 000 km

Sources: World Bank; UNDP; HCR; MSF; WFP.

Famine is not a specifically African phenomenon, even though the main famines in the last 30 years have occurred in sub-Saharan Africa. Famine is an acute symptom of the political and economic crises affecting most African countries. It can also sometimes be the result of deliberate policies.

Principal famines in the last 30 years

◆

Biafra, 1968: the conflict between the Ibo independence movement and the Nigerian army, together with the drought, caused between 500,000 and 2 million victims, most of whom starved.

Sahel, 1972-75: a drought caused chronic malnutrition and famine. This resulted in several hundred thousand victims.

Ethiopia, 1973-74: a major drought; because of the authorities' failure to react, the ensuing famine killed several hundred thousand people.

Ethiopia, 1984-85: the drought and the consequences of the conflict between Colonel Mengistu's regime and the Eritrean and Ethiopian guerilla fighters caused a famine that killed several hundred thousand people, mostly in the conflict zones in northern Ethiopia.

Mozambique, 1986: drought in southern Africa. The conflict between Renamo and Frelimo in Mozambique turned food shortages into famine in several particularly vulnerable regions.

Sudan, 1984-85: a drought triggered famine.

South Sudan, 1988-90: a drought worsened in South Sudan while more than 2 million people were displaced by the fighting and the assistance operation was held up by the authorities. The number of famine victims was estimated at more than 250,000.

South Sudan, Mozambique and Somalia, 1992-93: a drought occurred in all the southern and eastern African countries. More than 18 million persons were at risk of malnutrition. Real famines occurred only in three countries: South Sudan, Mozambique and especially Somalia, all three countries ravaged by war.

Angola, Liberia and South Sudan, 1994: famine areas were recorded in these countries; none was experiencing a drought; all were affected by conflicts.

THE FAMINE IN ANGOLA

A famine situation is always an exceptional phenomenon. The case of Angola is representative of the food emergency situations of recent years. This shows that emergencies are less linked to drought than to the consequences of war.

Angola is rich in natural resources, and in most areas rainfall is adequate for agriculture.

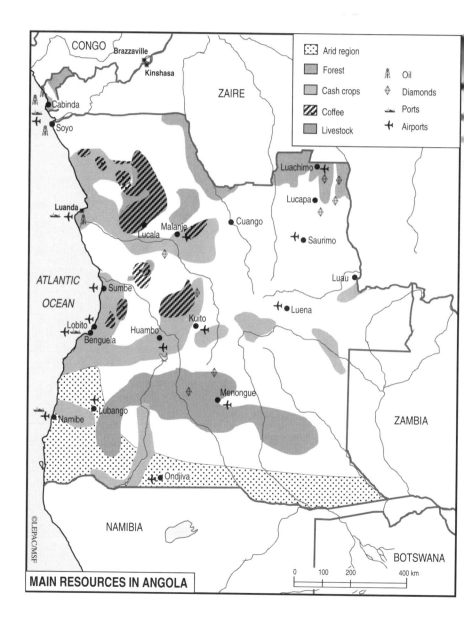

MAIN RESOURCES IN ANGOLA

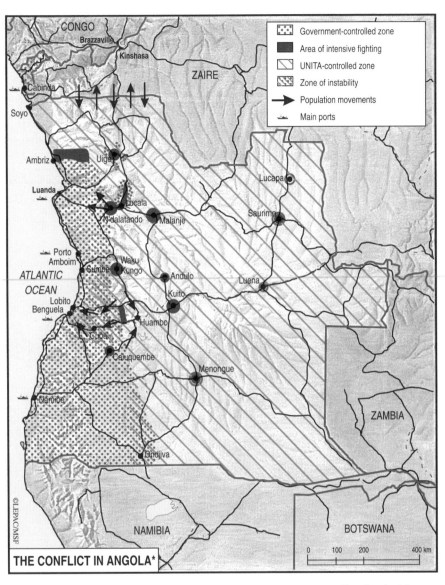

THE CONFLICT IN ANGOLA*

Legend:
- Government-controlled zone
- Area of intensive fighting
- UNITA-controlled zone
- Zone of instability
- Population movements
- Main ports

©LEPAC/MSF

Sources: WFP; MSF.   * Situation in July 1994

As the peace process was getting under way, UNITA (National Union for the Total Independence of Angola), having rejected the electoral results in September 1992, renewed its war against the government of the MPLA (People's Movement for the Liberation of Angola). The conflict once again split the country in two and trapped many towns, isolating or displacing a large segment of the population.

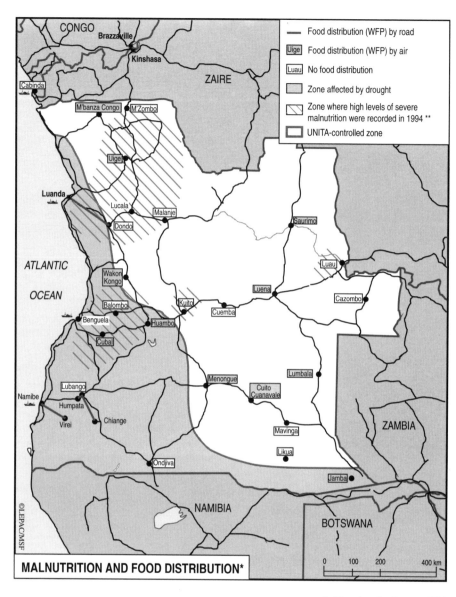

MALNUTRITION AND FOOD DISTRIBUTION*

Legend:
- Food distribution (WFP) by road
- Uige Food distribution (WFP) by air
- Luau No food distribution
- Zone affected by drought
- Zone where high levels of severe malnutrition were recorded in 1994 **
- UNITA-controlled zone

* Situation in August 1994

** Among the regions affected by malnutrition in Angola, only those to which the humanitarian organizations had access are indicated on the map.

Although the World Food Programme established a programme for the distribution of food by air, the fighting and the protagonists themselves regularly prevented access to many towns. With supplies interrupted, famine ensued in certain areas. Since the resumption of the conflict, famine has been responsible for as many if not more victims than the fighting itself.

15

EPIDEMICS

An epidemic is the name given to the sudden appearance of numerous cases of a disease, or a considerable increase in the number of cases of a specific disease in a given region.

The most serious epidemics in the southern hemisphere are:

Measles. — In the absence of vaccination, measles can kill between 10 and 20 percent of children infected.

Cholera. — In the absence of rapid treatment in rehydration centres, cholera can lead to the deaths of nearly half a given population.

Shigellosis (bleeding diarrhoea). — This disease is particularly difficult to treat owing to its resistance to the most common antibiotics and the high cost of acquiring the more effective medicines. Shigellosis can infect up to a third of a given population and can lead to death in the cases of between 5 and 10 percent.

Meningitis. — In the absence of a speedy vaccination campaign, meningitis has a dramatic affect on communities and can lead to death in between 10 and 20 percent of cases.

Conflict often has a direct bearing on the appearance or spread of epidemics. It can contribute to the disorganization of the health system, which complicates prevention and treatment and, in so doing, leads to the spread of disease. Conflict can also hinder access to an infected population which can, in turn, delay treatment. Conflict can also lead to the displacement and regrouping of populations in situations where poor hygiene can increase transmission. Finally, displaced people, who are often impoverished and suffering from malnutrition, have a heightened vulnerability to disease.

MALARIA AND ITS RESISTANCE WORLDWIDE

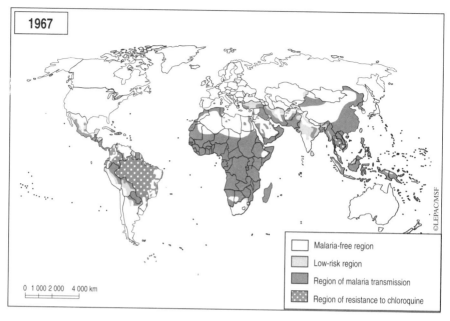

Source: WHO.

Malaria: a disease endemic to most tropical regions caused by parasitic protozoans in the red blood cells transmitted by the bite of anopheles (mosquitoes). The disease is characterised by periodic attacks of fever. The most severe forms of malaria lead to coma, followed by death.

In spite of efforts to eradicate this disease totally in the 1950s by means of insecticides, malaria today presents the most serious problem of all transmissible diseases. The situation world-wide has deteriorated since 1970. The annual toll is now estimated at between 300 to 500 million, and there are an estimated 1.5 to 3 million deaths every year. Major epidemics occur regularly in Africa and Asia. These epidemics are linked to the increasing resistance of mosquitoes to insecticides, and to their growing resistance to medicines such as chloroquine, as well as to environmental changes and conflicts and their impact (Burma, Vietnam, Cambodia).

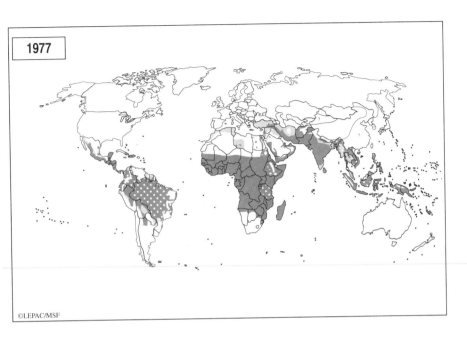

1977

©LEPAC/MSF

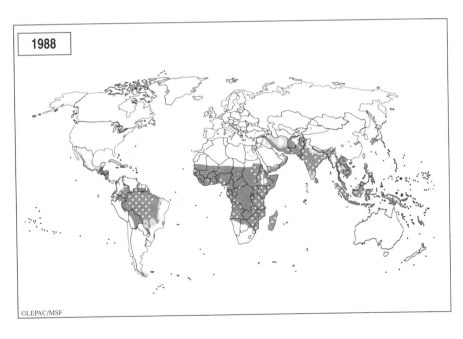

1988

©LEPAC/MSF

EPIDEMIC OF HELIOTROPE POISONING
IN TAJIKISTAN

Bread is the staple food of the Tajik people living in the Farkhar region (98,000 inhabitants). It is made from wheat, traditionally sent by the Russian collective farms in the region to the central plant in Dushanbe, where it is processed into flour. In 1992, this circuit was interrupted when the conflict between the pro-Communist forces and the Islamic-Democrat coalition worsened towards the end of the summer and became concentrated geographically in the south-western part of the country, in particular near and south of Kourgan Tiube. From 5 May to 15 November, owing to the lack of security, the Farkhar region was subjected to a total blockade, causing severe food shortages and a delay in agricultural work. The wheat harvest is normally brought in by July, but that year was not brought in until September. That summer there was a drought in southern Tajikistan which provoked the growth of heliotrope, a poisonous plant that grows, blossoms and goes to seed in the region's wheat fields. Owing to the delay in the harvest, the heliotrope seeds were harvested along with the wheat. After the harvest, the wheat was placed in storage. Due to the blockade, the wheat was distributed to the population of the

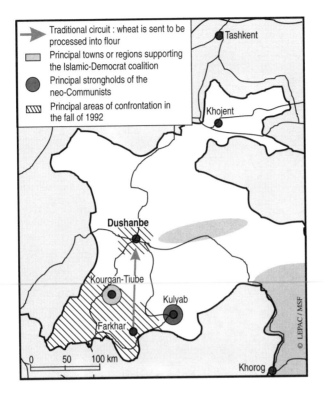

Legend:
- Traditional circuit : wheat is sent to be processed into flour
- Principal towns or regions supporting the Islamic-Democrat coalition
- Principal strongholds of the neo-Communists
- Principal areas of confrontation in the fall of 1992

Tashkent

Khojent

Dushanbe

Kourgan-Tiube

Kulyab

Farkhar

0   50   100 km

Khorog

© LEPAC / MSF

Source: Epicentre.

collective farms, whom, given the exceptional conditions, had to mill their own flour and make their own bread. On 15 October, the first case of heliotrope food poisoning was recorded in the Farkhar region. Even after it was confirmed in November that the contamination was caused by the presence of heliotrope seeds in the wheat, the population continued eating the contaminated bread because of the severe food shortages in the region. Consequently, the epidemic spread rapidly, affecting 3,906 persons.

The end of the war, in mid-November, and the resumption of trade with the capital, enabled the Tajik government to set up a programme to replace the contaminated flour in mid-December. The epidemic ended in early March 1993.

16

SUDAN:
A CASE STUDY

The Sudanese crisis is, without a doubt, one of the most serious in recent years. For the past ten years, the southern part of the country has been a stage on which a human tragedy has been played out. In Sudan, all the factors leading to crisis explored in the preceding chapters are intermingled and mutually reinforced.

The war, which is ravaging the southern part of the country, has led to the massive displacement of people who flee the killing and military attacks. The fighting and insecurity have had an adverse affect on farming and have interrupted regional trade. This has led to chronic food shortages and famine. Moreover, the work of aid agencies is continually held up not only by the insecurity but by the unwillingness of the authorities to facilitate the provision of aid to those suspected of sympathising with the enemy. This policy of withholding food aid has not only led to further displacement of people who leave their regions in search of food, but has also accelerated the spread of kala-azar. This disease, which has yet to be controlled, has already produced numerous victims whose numbers can be added to those who have succumbed to war, massacre and famine.

AGRICULTURE AND MAIN ETHNIC GROUPS
IN SUDAN

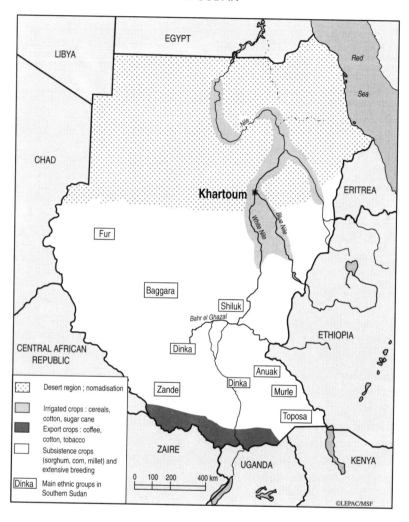

Sudan has a great agricultural potential, but its wealth is distributed unequally. The country is divided into three climatic zones: a northern desert region, a central band of cultivated savannahs prone to flooding, and a southern region of wooded savannahs. Irrigated fertile zones are found on both sides of the two Niles. In its time, Sudan was known as "the breadbasket of the Arab world" because of its agricultural wealth. The map also indicates a complex ethno-linguistic distribution: in the north are Arab or Arab-speaking populations and in the south Negro-African populations.

CONFLICT, DROUGHT AND DISPLACED PEOPLE IN SOUTH SUDAN

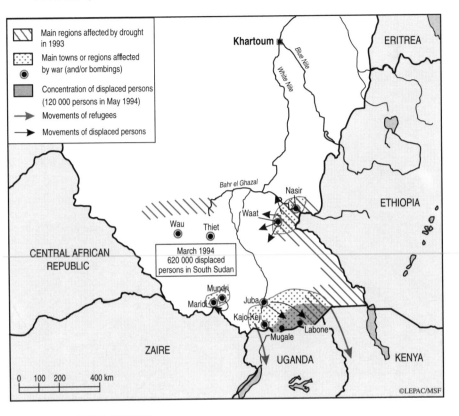

Sources: MSF; FEWS (USAID).

Since 1983, these ethno-linguistic divisions have contributed to the conflict between government forces and the Sudan People's Liberation Army. Added to these clashes are the conflicts between the different factions making up the People's Army. Concentrated in the southern part of the country, the fighting and massacres have given rise to hundreds of thousands of victims and displaced persons who seek refuge on the outskirts of towns in the hope of finding safety and the food aid on which their survival depends.

In 1993, a drought occurred in several areas of South Sudan, which had already been ravaged by conflict. The lack of rainfall aggravated the consequences of war and population movements. Continuing insecurity interrupted regional trade, had an adverse affect on agriculture at crucial moments and contributed to the fall in cereal production and the availability of food stocks for the impoverished displaced people.

MALNUTRITION AND EPIDEMICS IN SOUTH SUDAN

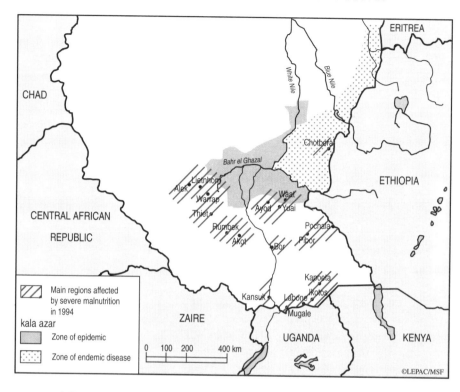

In addition to the victims of war, massacres and displacements, Sudan has also many victims of famine. The Sudanese government has long since used food as a weapon to weaken and even decimate populations suspected of sympathizing with the Sudan People's Liberation Army. Humanitarian organizations are refused access to vast areas and others are so dangerous that food can only be distributed by means of uncertain air drops.

In the wake of the civil war, which destroyed health structures, and the displacement and regrouping of populations, there was an outbreak of kala-azar in 1984 in the upper Nile region. Since populations are not accessible, no real control is possible in the epidemic areas, which in 1994 are still spreading to the northern and southern parts of the country. In the zones most affected by fighting, which were inaccessible to humanitarian organizations, this parasitical disease, spread by a sand fly and fatal in a matter of months, is said to have already contaminated more than 50,000 persons.

Médecins Sans Frontières

Médecins Sans Frontières is a private, non-profit, international organization, whose objective is to provide medical aid to populations in crisis, without discrimination.

The organization relies on volunteer health professionals and is independent of all States or institutions, as well as of all political, economic or religious influences.

MSF was established in 1971 by doctors determined to offer emergency assistance wherever wars and man-made disasters occur in the world. Its guiding principles are laid down in a charter to which all members of the organization subscribe.

During more than 20 years of relief work around the world, Médecins Sans Frontières has gained a wide range of expertise, tested techniques and strategies of intervention that allow it to pool rapidly the logistics and human resources necessary to provide efficient aid.

Largely supported by private donors, the organization is able to maintain great interventional flexibility and total independence in its choice of operations.

Moreover, in bearing witness to violations of basic humanitarian principles and denouncing them publicly, Médecins Sans Frontières volunteers implement a vital part of their humanitarian commitment.

The international Médecins Sans Frontières network is made up of six operational sections (France, Belgium, Holland, Spain, Luxembourg and Switzerland), and delegate offices in twelve countries. An international office, based in Brussels, is responsible for liaising with international organizations.

In 1994, 3,000 Médecins Sans Frontières
of 45 different nationalities worked in 80 countries.

The Charter
of
Médecins Sans Frontières

Médecins Sans Frontières is a private international organization. Most of its members are doctors and health workers, but many other support professions contribute to MSF's smooth functioning. All of them agree to honour the following principles:

- Médecins Sans Frontières offers assistance to populations in distress, to victims of natural or man-made disasters and to victims of armed conflict, without discrimination and irrespective of race, religion, creed or political affiliation.

- Médecins Sans Frontières observes strict neutrality and impartiality in the name of universal medical ethics and the right to humanitarian assistance and demands full and unhindered freedom in the exercise of its functions.

- Médecins Sans Frontières's volunteers undertake to respect their professional code of ethics and to maintain complete independence from all political, economic and religious powers.

- As volunteers, members are aware of the risks and dangers of the missions they undertake, and have no right to compensation for themselves or their beneficiaries other than that which Médecins Sans Frontières is able to afford them.

MÉDECINS SANS FRONTIÈRES WORLDWIDE

OPERATIONAL SECTIONS

Belgium
Médecins Sans Frontières
Artsen zonder Grenzen
Rue Dupré 94
B-1090 Bruxelles
Tel. 32-2-474 74 74
Fax 32-2-474 74 70

France
Médecins Sans Frontières
8, rue Saint-Sabin
F-75011 Paris
Tel. 33-1-40 21 29 29
Fax 33-1-48 06 26 87

Holland
Médecins Sans Frontières
Artsen zonder Grenzen
Max Euweplein 40
NL-1001 EA Amsterdam
Tel. 31-20-52 08 700
Fax 31-20-620 51 70

Luxembourg
Médecins Sans Frontières
70, Route de Luxembourg
L-7240 Bereldange
Tel. 352-33 25 15
Fax 353-33 51 07

Spain
Médecins Sans Frontières
Medicos Sin Fronteras
Nou de la Rambla 26
E-08001 Barcelona
Tel. 34-3-304 61 00
Fax 34-3-304 61 02

Switzerland
Médecins Sans Frontières
3, Clos de la Fonderie
CH-1227 Carouge / Genève
Tel. 41-22-300 44 45
Fax 41-22-318 50 24

BRANCH OFFICES

Australia
Médecins Sans Frontières
28 Levey Street
Chippendale NSW 2008
GPO Box 5141 Sydney 2001
Tel. 61-2-319 35 00
Fax 61-2-319 23 83

Austria
Médecins Sans Frontières
Ärzte ohne Grenzen
Gumpendorferstrasse 95
A-1060 Wien
Tel. 43-1-59 30 39 00
Fax 43-1-59 60 390 10

Canada
Médecins Sans Frontières
Doctors Without Borders
51 Front East 2nd Floor
Toronto, Ontario m5E 1B3
Tel. 416-366 67 02
Fax 416-366 94 25

Denmark
Médecins Sans Frontières
Laeger uden Graenser
Strandvejen 171,1
DK-2900 Hellerup
Tel. 45-31-62 63 01
Fax 45-39-40 14 92

Germany
Médecins Sans Frontières
Ärzte ohne Grenzen
Adenauer Allee 50
D-53113 Bonn
Tel. 49-228-91 46 70
Fax 49-228-91 46 711

Greece
Médecins Sans Frontières
Giatri Horis Synora
11 rue Paioniou
GR-10440 Athens
Tel. 30-1-88 35 334
Fax 30-1-88 29 988

Hong Kong
Médecins Sans Frontières
GPO Box 5803
Hong Kong
Tel. 852-338 82 77
Fax 852-304 60 81

Italy
Médecins Sans Frontières
Medici senza Frontiere
Via Ostiense 6/E
I-00154 Roma
Tel. 39-6-57 300 900
Fax 39-6-57 300 902

Japan
Médecins Sans Frontières
Takadanobaba 3-8-27
Shinjuku-Ku
Tokyo 169
Tel. 81-3-3366 8571
Fax 81-3-3366 8573

Sweden
Médecins Sans Frontières
Läkare utan Gränser
Vulkcanusgatan 8
S-11321 Stockholm
Tel. 46-8-31 02 17
Fax 46-8-31 42 90

United Kingdom
Médecins Sans Frontières
124-132 Clerkenwell Road
EC1R 5DL London
Tel. 44-71-713 56 00
Fax 44-71-713 50 04

United States
Médecins Sans Frontières
Doctors Without Borders
30 Rockefeller Plaza
Suite 5425
New York NY 10112

Composition Facompo à Lisieux
Achevé d'imprimer sur les presses de
MAME IMPRIMEURS, à Tours. Dépôt légal Janvier 1995
ISBN 0-9525057-0-3.

LA DÉCOUVERTE